W9-BVC-199

Beads And Cabochons:
How To Create Fashion Earrings and Jewelry

Written and Illustrated by

Patricia Lyman

WITHDRAWN

Tribal Library
Saginaw Chippewa Indian Tribe
7070 E. Broadway
Mt. Pleasant MI 48858

Copyright © MCMXCII by Eagle's View Publishing

All rights reserved. No part of this book may be reproduced or transmitted in any form or by any means, electronic or mechanical, including, but not restricted to, photocopying, recording, or using any information storage or retrieval system, without permission in writing from the publisher.

Eagle's View Publishing Company
6756 North Fork Road
Liberty, UT 84310

ISBN: 0-943604-32-X
Library of Congress Catalog Card Number: 90-86227

FIRST EDITION

DEDICATION

I dedicate this book to my family:
To my daughter Ara and my son Travis who have helped me so much.

10 9 8 7 6 5 4 3 2 1

TABLE OF CONTENTS

ACKNOWLEDGEMENTS

I wish to thank all the friends who have inspired and encouraged me to write this book, including my mother and father. I also wish to thank my editor, Denise Knight, and Kris Sweat and Brenda Jensen who proofed the manuscript and made suggestions.

ABOUT THE AUTHOR

Patricia Lyman is a lady of high energy and many skills who learned needlecraft as a child and has practiced it all her life. After conquering goat cheese and organic gardening, she discovered the medium of glass beads and became completely enthralled. She became an expert beadworker and started creating her own designs in a short period of time. Many of them build on classic Native American designs, but she has gone beyond this to create unique combinations of semiprecious stones, quills and crystals that are elegant, exciting and different. Her work has won several awards at art shows.

Patricia lives with her two children, Ara and Travis. They have a log cabin on the banks of the beautiful Kettle River in the Cascade Mountains of northeastern Washington. The family's living comes from their craftwork.

INTRODUCTION

Since I first started beading, many people have wanted to learn to make my various designs. Sharing my knowledge has been one of the most rewarding aspects of doing beadwork. I have made many friends this way and I hope to make many more by sharing my knowledge through this book.

This book can be useful to both the beginning beader and to those with more experience. The use of cabochons and other semiprecious stones in beaded jewelry is unique and original. A few of the projects are new variations on common earring techniques that should also stimulate new creativity. Many of the techniques used will be new to most beaders.

To use this book, look through the pictures and choose a pleasing design. Read the instructions for this project and assemble the needed supplies. While working, read the directions for each step and look at the illustrations. Visualize the work involved and then complete the step. Leave the work long enough to read the next step thoroughly, then continue.

Each section teaches a different technique, which is explained in detail and illustrated with many helpful diagrams in the instructions at the beginning of the section. The projects at the beginning of each section are the easiest and show how the information provided in the instructions is used in the context of an actual piece of beadwork. Later projects, although designed to stand alone, often assume these techniques are familiar. Craftworkers starting with a project in the middle of a section may want to read through the earlier projects and instructions before beginning work. Everyone should read the Materials and General Instructions sections, both for the information they contain and to become familiar with terms and techniques which are used throughout the book.

Finally, each project features one of the many possible color schemes for that design. Alternate color schemes are usually suggested, but do not hesitate to use entirely different colors, change the beads used or alter the designs themselves. Personalized creations are what beading is all about. Select colors that complement your wardrobe, the wardrobe of a friend, or which match the newest trends in fashion.

MATERIALS

The tools and supplies used in this book are discussed in this section. A list of required materials is also given at the start of each project. Some items should be on hand for all the projects; these are marked with an asterisk (*) in this section and they are not listed again. Example color schemes are used for each project, but the possible combinations are endless and should be explored.

Beads: Beads are sold loose in bags or plastic containers, or on strings in bunches called "hanks". The number of beads per ounce or hank varies according to bead size.

Beads vary slightly in diameter, thickness and hole size. Some beads in every batch are irregular in shape or vary too much from the "average size" and must be discarded. When buying beads, look for those which are relatively uniform in size and shape. The most uniform beads are sold in hanks, but the uniformity of loose beads has greatly improved in recent years and the price is usually better.

An entire hank of any one color is not needed for any project in this book, however there will be discards, and it can be difficult to match beads made in different lots. Not only does the size vary, but the exact color is often different from one dye batch to another. Therefore, always purchase more beads than it seems will be needed. Unless specified, purchase at least a half ounce of each color of seed bead for the projects in this book. When the number of beads is specified for a project, this is the number in the finished piece(s), so be sure to purchase extras.

Several types of beads are used in this book. A brief description of these is given here for the benefit of the novice.

Seed beads are small round glass beads. They come in numbered sizes and the larger the number, the smaller the bead. They are made from translucent (see through) or opaque glass in a wide variety of colors and many different finishes are added to the glass (pearl, luster, iris, etc.). One hank of size 12/° seed beads is usually slightly more than one ounce of loose beads and a hank of size 10/° beads is usually slightly less than two ounces. Rocailles are beads lined with silver. Cut seed beads have small flat areas, or facets, cut on the surface of the bead which add sparkle and shine.

Bugle beads are small elongated glass cylinders ranging from 1/8 inch to 1 1/2 inches in length. Size 3 bugle beads are 5/16 inch in length. Bugle beads are also made in a wide variety of colors and finishes.

Stone beads are made from precious or semiprecious stones, such as turquoise, jade, onyx, and garnet. They have a hole drilled through them and are sized by the diameter of the bead in millimeters (mm); 3 to 5 mm beads are best suited for earrings. Other types of beads come in colors designated with the names of these stones, e.g. turquoise. To avoid confusion, these colors will be designated as turquoise blue, jade green, etc. and the semi precious beads will be referred to as turquoise stone, jade stone, etc.

Crystal faceted beads come in many shapes. They are cut from Austrian leaded glass crystal and are sized by the diameter of the bead at its widest point, in millimeters. Tapered or rondelle crystals are used in this book to add striking beauty and texture to earrings.

Pony or E beads are larger than seed beads. They are sized by the same system and usually come in sizes 5/° and 6/°.

Cabochons: Cabochons are polished pieces of precious or semiprecious stone which are domed on the top and flat on the bottom. Cabochons that are circular or oval in shape are used in this book. Sizes indicate the diameter of circular stones (e.g. 5 mm round) or the lengths of the two axes of oval stones (e.g. 10 mm x 12 mm). Look for stones with very high domes and flat backs. For earrings or jewelry sets, choose stones as similar in appearance as possible.

Stone Crystals: Some stones, such as quartz or amethyst, form natural crystals with characteristic shapes. These can be used to make very distinctive pieces of jewelry. Crystals of any size can be used for necklaces, while crystals about an inch long work best for earrings. For beginners, symmetrical, pencil shaped crystals with smooth sides are a good choice. Irregular crystals or crystal clusters can be attractively beaded by those with more experience. Crystals for earrings should match as closely as possible.

Porcupine Quills: Porcupine quills are white or cream in color, with a black tip and they add a unique touch and change of texture to jewelry projects. Quills can be used in place of bugle beads in many of the designs. The tips are sharp and can be dangerous so they must be handled with care.

Thread: White "nymo" or nylon thread is the preferred thread for beaded jewelry. Sizes A and B are used in this book, with A being the finer of the two. Nymo stretches when pulled, but this can be adjusted for quite easily. Nymo comes in bobbins, spools and three ounce cones. The cone thread generally requires less waxing and shrinks less.

*Beeswax: Beading thread should be coated with beeswax to prevent knots and tangles and to protect the thread from being cut by the sharp edges of some beads. This is done by running the thread across the beeswax with a twisting motion. Add enough wax to eliminate tangles, but not so much that the wax comes off when the thread is pulled through the beads.

Needles: Needles made specifically for the purpose are required for beading. There are two types: Beading or Long beading needles, and Short or Sharps beading needles. They come in numbered sizes and the smaller the number, the larger or thicker the needle. English beading needle sizes are used in this book. They correspond to seed bead sizes of the same number, but thinner (higher number) needles are usually used as the thread often must go through a single bead several times. Needles tend to break while beading, so always have extras on hand.

Glover's needles are used to pierce holes in the leather backing used on many of the pieces. A heavy sewing needle will also come in handy for positioning knots on necklace clasps.

*Scissors: A good sharp pair of needle-nosed scissors is indispensable. Use whatever size is most comfortable, but most people prefer small ones for this kind of work.

*Pliers: Needle-nosed pliers with wire cutters are needed for attaching the metal findings to the earrings and necklaces. The inside of the tips should be serrated for a good grip. Bent tip pliers also come in handy when working with findings.

*Ruler: Straight guidelines are necessary for good beadwork.

*Marking Pen and Pencil: An indelible ink marking pen with a razor or ultra fine point and a pencil are needed to mark beading points and draw guidelines.

*Clear Fingernail Polish: Fingernail polish is used to coat knots so they will not slip, to stiffen solid areas of beadwork, and to secure thread ends woven into the beadwork.

*Containers: Small, shallow containers, such as mayonnaise jar lids are needed to hold beads while working. Zip lock bags (2" x 3") are great for storing beads between projects. A funnel can be used to get the beads into the zip lock bags.

The following supplies are needed, in addition to the above items, for the cabochon jewelry projects.

*Pellon: Cabochons are glued to fabric and the beads are then stitched around the stones. Use white pellon stabilizer interfacing for heavy fabrics, #50 or #65. Buy enough to fit in the embroidery hoop being used. An eight inch square of pellon is enough for a six inch diameter hoop.

*Earring Wire
Figure 1-2*

*Embroidery Hoop: The pellon is placed in an embroidery hoop for beading. A six to ten inch diameter hoop is needed and wooden ones work best.

*Glue: The best glue for securing the cabochons to the pellon and the findings to the beadwork is the "Amazing Welder" made by Nybco. It is also sold under the names "Shoe Goo" and "Household Goop".

Leather: Thin leather, 1/32 to 1/16 inch thick, is used to back all of the cabochon jewelry projects. Choose colors which match or complement the beadwork.

Plastic: Thin plastic pieces are used for stiffness in the cabochon projects which do not have earring posts. They can be cut from plastic milk jugs or similar containers which have been thoroughly washed.

*Styrofoam: A clean piece of styrofoam, 6" x 6" and at least one inch thick is needed to mount the leather backing on cabochon pieces with earring posts.

Bead Stringing Kit: Bead stringing kits contain six and a half feet of either nylon or silk cord, which is heavier than beading thread. The heavier cord is used for beaded necklace strings, because it is stronger. The kits come with a needle already attached to one end of the cord. This is important, because the cord will not fit through seed beads if it is strung on a beading needle.

Findings: Findings are the materials, such as earring wires, necklace clasps and pin backs, which finished beadwork is mounted on to create jewelry. Common earring findings are

*Earring Hooks
Figure 1-1*

*Earring Posts
Figure 1-3*   *Figure 1-4*

illustrated in Figures 1-1 to 1-4. Many variations of these basic findings are available. Substitutions, based on personal preference or availability, are often possible; use common sense and the advice of professionals to determine what is appropriate.

Earring findings are made from a variety of metals and usually, the higher the quality, the higher the price. The higher quality findings are worth the price in appearance and longevity.

Sources: Most of these supplies are available from general craft stores, Indian craft stores or trading posts. If they do not have them, they can usually get them or suggest other suppliers. Pellon is available at fabric stores, the glue and epoxy can be found at hardware stores, and stone beads and cabochons can be found at jewelers who deal in stones. Places which cut stones are called lapidaries, so try this in the yellow pages.

GENERAL INSTRUCTIONS

To use this book effectively, first browse through the pages and select a project whose design is appealing. Decide on the color combinations to be used, read the materials section for hints and then gather the materials needed. Begin by reading the general instructions section to become familiar with the terms and techniques used in this book. Then read the appropriate section instructions and the specific project directions completely before starting to bead. If necessary, review the general instructions again.

Work on a flat surface at a comfortable height, with plenty of room for bead containers and tools. Cover the surface with a clean cloth or felt. The area must be well lighted. An adjustable lamp over the work area, with at least a 100 watt bulb, is a great help in avoiding eye strain. In the daytime, working near a bright window also helps, but does not replace the lamp. Eyestrain can also be avoided by taking a break and resting tired eyes.

Before starting a project, place the beads, loose, in shallow bowls or mayonnaise jar lids. This allows the beads to be easily sorted through while beading and makes them easy to pick up with the needle.

While working, read each step and look at the illustrations to visualize the process before beginning. Once a step is completed, pause and read the next step before continuing.

Knots and Thread

The **thread length** used for beading should be what is comfortable and manageable for the

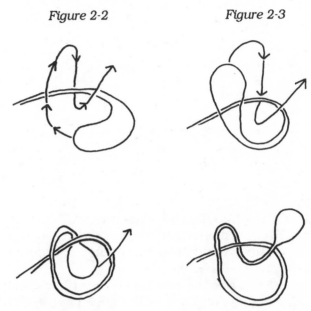

Figure 2-2   *Figure 2-3*

Figure 2-4   *Figure 2-5*

individual beader, but about 3 feet is a good starting point. Run the thread over a piece of beeswax to take the curl out of it and prevent tangles. All the projects in this book use a single thread, so pull about a third of the thread through the needle (Figure 2-1). Do not knot the thread unless the project directions call for it, and then be sure to use the knot specified.

Several knots are used throughout this book and they are described in detail here. Practice those which are unfamiliar before beginning a project. All the knots should be coated with clear fingernail polish after they are tightened to

Figure 2-1

Figure 2-6   *Figure 2-7*

prevent them from slipping.

The **loop knot** has many beading applications. To make the basic knot, double the end of the thread back on itself for about six inches (Figure 2-2). Bring the loop end of the thread up and over the doubled thread (Figure 2-3), then back through the circle this creates (Figures 2-4

Figure 2-12　　　　　*Figure 2-13*

Figure 2-14

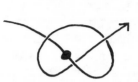

Figure 2-8

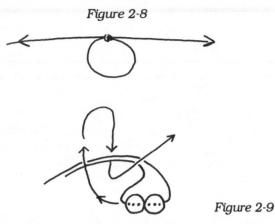

Figure 2-9

to 2-5). Tighten the thread down into a knot, leaving a loop in the end of the thread (Figures 2-6 and 2-7). If more tightening is needed, pull the two threads coming out of the knot in opposite directions (Figure 2-8).

A **loop knot** can be made with varying numbers and styles of beads trapped in the loop at the end of the thread (Figures 2-9 to 2-11). String the beads on the thread, placing them about six inches from the end. Double the end of the thread on itself, creating a loop with the beads in the center of it. Bring the beads up and over the doubled thread, then back through the circle this

Figure 2-10

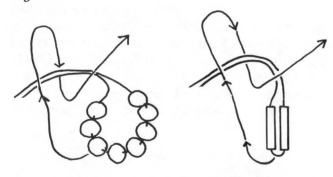

Figure 2-11

creates. Move the knot down the thread, snug against the beads, and tighten it by pulling the two thread ends in opposite directions.

An **anchor knot** is used to secure the end

of a single thread at the beginning of beadwork on pellon. It is essentially a loop knot tied in one thread instead of two, but three knots are stacked over one another to make it larger. To tie this knot, make a loop in the end of the thread. Bring the end of the thread through the loop (Figure 2-12). As the knot is pulled tight, maneuver it to a spot that is about two inches from the end of the thread. Tie a second knot in the same way as the first (Figure 2-13), maneuvering the new knot to sit on top of the first one. The idea is to make one larger knot, rather than two knots next to one another. Tie a third knot (Figure 2-14) on top of the other two. An anchor knot must be big enough that it will not pull through the pellon, so if thin thread (size A or thinner) is used, a fourth knot may be necessary.

A **square knot** is usually used to tie off two thread ends. This knot requires less thread to tie than a loop knot, so it can be used in a tight spot to add on new thread. To tie it, wrap one of the

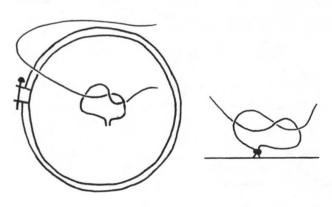

Figure 2-15　　　　　*Figure 2-16*

Figure 2-17

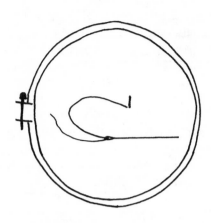

Figure 2-24

complete the knot. The "rule" for remembering this knot is "right over left, then left over right", referring to the starting positions of the two thread ends from which the knot is tied.

A **finishing knot** is used to secure the end of the thread on the back of pellon or leather, after a portion of the beadwork is finished. Start with the needle and thread on the back of the beadwork,

Figure 2-25

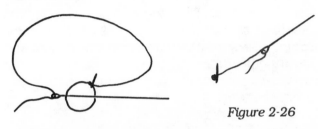

Figure 2-26

thread ends around the other (Figure 2-15), then pull the thread ends in opposite directions to tighten this half of the knot. Next, wrap the second thread end around the first one (Figure 2-16) and pull the ends in opposite directions to

Figure 2-18   *Figure 2-19*

Figure 2-20   *Figure 2-21*

Figure 2-22   *Figure 2-23*

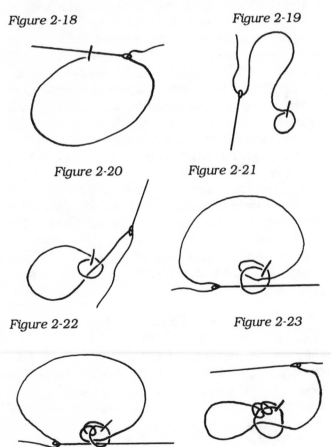

right next to a previous stitch (Figure 2-17). If there is no previous stitch, then take a small stitch in the material. Run the needle under the thread of the previous stitch (Figure 2-18), pulling the thread through until a loop about the size of a pencil remains (Figure 2-19). Run the needle through this loop three times, wrapping the thread around the loop thread (Figures 2-20 to 2-22). The third time through, leave a new pencil sized loop (Figure 2-23). Grasp this new loop and pull on it until the first loop and the rest of the thread is pulled tight (Figure 2-24). Run the needle

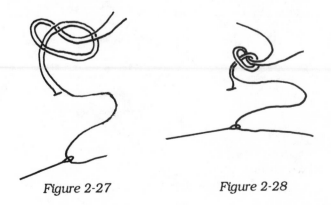

Figure 2-27   *Figure 2-28*

7

through the new loop once (Figure 2-25) and pull the knot tight, loop and all (Figure 2-26).

Two techniques may be used to **add new thread** if it runs short while beading. If the beading is on pellon or leather, a new piece of thread can be tied to the old one on the back of the work, using a loop knot. Make a final stitch with the old thread, so that the needle and thread are on the underside of the beadwork, then remove the needle. Cut a new length of thread. The needle can be put on the new thread now or after the knot is made. Put the two ends of the threads together and treat them as the loop end in the loop knot. Bring the ends over the two pieces of thread and back through the circle this creates (Figure 2-27). Move the knot as close to the pellon as possible, then tighten it against the back of the work by pulling the two thread ends in opposite directions (Figure 2-28). The knot must be tight against the pellon so that the previous stitching does not loosen. Tie a square knot on top of the loop knot and trim off the excess short threads. Coat the knot with clear fingernail polish and continue beading.

Figure 2-29

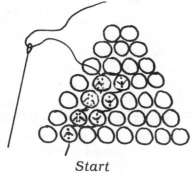

Start

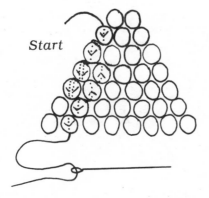

Start

Figure 2-30

If the beading is not on material, then the short end of the thread is simply woven up and down through about 10 beads in the work and any excess thread clipped off (Figure 2-29). Make sure to do this before the thread gets too short. A new piece of thread is started by weaving it through another 10 or so beads, then back to where the work left off (Figure 2-30). If a bead is too tight for the needle to go through, take the needle off the thread and slip on a thinner needle (higher number) to finish securing the thread, then switch back to the regular needle. Make sure these areas are coated with fingernail polish when the piece is finished.

Beading Tips

Quality beadwork has a neat, even, consistent appearance which is produced by a combination of skill, art and intuition. The instructions in this book seek, for the most part, to teach skills. This section, while adding new skills, also seeks to indicate where art and intuition become involved and when to use them. The message is - do not be afraid to do what looks and feels right, even if it does not match the instructions exactly.

Many of the projects in this book have a design, made of different color beads, incorporated into the beadwork. Maintaining crisp definition of the design elements is more important than using the exact number of beads called for in the instructions for each project. There are several ways to make sure that the design is properly executed.

The foundations of good design execution are accurately placed and drawn guidelines. Distances must be exact and straight lines must really be straight. Curves should be as smooth as possible and points should be sharp. Good guidelines make it easier to bead the design crisply; without them, neat designs are impossible.

The fact that beads vary slightly in thickness is both the root of the problem and the solution. Three techniques can be used to adjust the beading and maintain the design: (1) If the beads do not meet the guidelines exactly, their positions can be adjusted slightly by the location of the stitches which secure them to the pellon. (2) Selecting the right size beads, that is choosing those which are thick or thin enough to fit the space available, and taking the time to substitute beads on the thread if necessary, is another solution. (3) In some cases it may be necessary to omit or add a bead to make the beads fit the design pattern. Two thin beads may fit better than one thick bead, two thick beads may work better than three thin ones, and so on; art and intuition as well as skill. Changes in bead number will be less noticeable if they are made in the background portion or color of the design.

An even appearance depends on the beads laying smoothly and snugly against one another. They should never appear crowded or bunchy. If no substitute can be found, it is better to leave a bead out than to cram it in where it will not fit properly.

The same principles apply to edging as well as bead patterns and designs. The even appearance of a loop edging is more important than skipping exactly two beads between each stitch. If thick beads in the outer row of the beadwork stretch the edging stitch too far, it may look better if only one bead in the outer row is skipped before running the needle under the connecting thread. Conversely, if the edging seems too bunchy due to thin beads in the outer row, skipping three beads before running the needle under the connecting thread may be the solution.

In all cases, watch the overall picture of the work as it progresses and make adjustments where necessary to accommodate the individuality of the beads and the pattern.

If a check of the work reveals an extra or wrong bead put in by mistake, there is an alternative to undoing everything back to that point. Take the needle nosed pliers and firmly grasp the incorrect bead in the tips. Make sure that the thread is <u>not</u> between the tips of the pliers or it will be cut. Squeeze the pliers and break the bead off the thread (Figure 2-31). If the wrong bead was used and the work is applique, sew a new single

bead directly to the pellon in its place. Beads which are not attached to material can not be replaced in this manner, but it is a great way to shorten a dangle which is too long.

Dangles

Many earring styles use a free hanging or dangling fringe on the bottom. The dangles are added to the foundation row beads of brick stitch and peyote stitch earrings, and they are stitched to the leather backing of cabochon jewelry. They are made by stringing beads on a single thread and then bringing the thread back through some, but not all, the beads in the dangle (Figure 2-32). It is important to get the proper tension in the thread running through the dangle. An overly tight dangle will look crooked and stiff, and the beads grinding against one another are prone to break the thread. Loose dangles will look sloppy, with thread showing between the beads and they are more prone to snag on things when the earring is worn. Also the tension in the thread must be the same coming up through the dangle as it is going down or the dangle will not hang straight.

Figure 2-32

To adjust the tension in the dangle, roll the beads at the bottom of the dangle between the fingers of one hand while pulling the thread snug

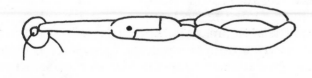

Figure 2-31

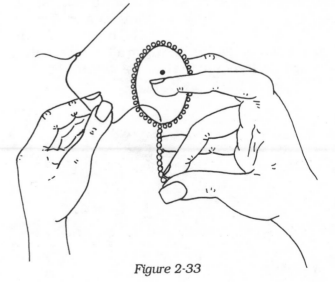

Figure 2-33

9

with the other hand (Figure 2-33). The beads should swing freely, but not be too loose. Experience will help in feeling the proper tension.

It is important that the dangles on either side of an earring have a uniform taper and also that the dangles on each earring in a pair be the same length. Keep in mind that differences in bead thickness can alter the lengths of the dangles so it may be necessary to add or omit a bead to get the desired length; do this in the portion of the design where it will be least noticeable.

Matching the taper from one side of the earring to the other can usually be done by eye, but matching the dangles on two separate earrings can be more difficult. One way to do this is to make a guide by placing the first earring on a piece of paper and marking the top of the earring and the bottom of each dangle. Compare each dangle on the second earring to the guide as it is made.

Figure 2-36

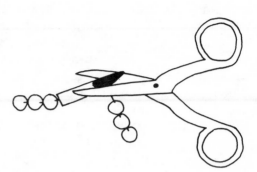

Figure 2-34

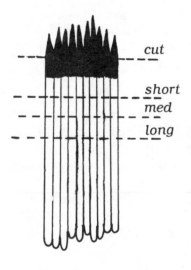

Working With Quills

Porcupine quills should be prepared at the beginning of the project in which they will be used, before beading begins. Quill tips can be dangerous, so be careful. If the quills are brittle, soak them for two minutes in warm water, then pat them dry. Take the porcupine quills and line them all up on a cutting board, dark ends at the top. Position the bottoms of the dark portions of the quills so that they are even with each other (Figure 2-34).

Using a sharp knife, cut off enough of the dark portions of the quills so that a needle will go through this end without splitting the quill. Keep the quills lined up and use the knife to cut the white ends of the quills to length all at once; this will ensure that the cut pieces are the same length. This length will vary depending on the dangle length desired.

The interior of porcupine quills is filled with a soft pith. The pith will give way easily, so to string a quill on the thread, just push the needle through as if it were any other bead being strung.

Earrings made with porcupine quills, which are being ruined because the thread through them is shrinking, can be salvaged. Bend the quill up and away from the thread that runs through it (Figure 2-35). If necessary, the thread can be used to cut through the quill enough to get the quill tip away from the thread. With sharp scissors, cut off a small piece of the quill, thus relieving the tension in the work (Figure 2-36).

Mounting Beadwork on Findings

Mounting beaded earrings on kidney shaped earring wires is quite simple. Open the wire latch, slip the attachment loop of the earring onto the wire, and pull it down into the wire loop at the bottom of the finding (Figure 2-37).

To mount earrings on French or Shepherds ear

Figure 2-37

Figure 2-35

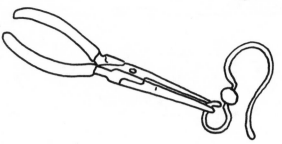

Figure 2-38

hooks, or on posts with drop rings, take the needle nosed pliers in one hand and one of the ear wires or posts in the other hand. With the pliers, grab the ring at the bottom of the ear wire or post, near the opening (Figure 2-38).

Twist the pliers to one side to pull the metal ring open (Figure 2-39). Hook the opened metal ring through the attachment loop at the top of the earring, making sure to catch all the threads (Figure 2-40). Use the pliers to twist the metal ring shut (Figure 2-41).

Earring pads with posts are glued to the back of flat portions of beaded earrings, either beaded cabochons or brick stitch triangles. Smear a thin even layer of glue on the flat side of the earring pad. Stick the glued side of the pad to the back of the earring, either on the pellon or to the beads themselves (Figure 2-42). On brick stitch work, place the pad at the top of the triangle; on round cabochons, center the pad on the back, using the stitches as a guideline; on oval cabochons, use the stitches as a guide and place the pad a little above center, so the earring will hang straighter when worn. Allow the glue to dry for at least an hour before continuing.

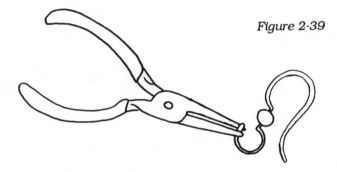

Figure 2-39

Figure 2-40

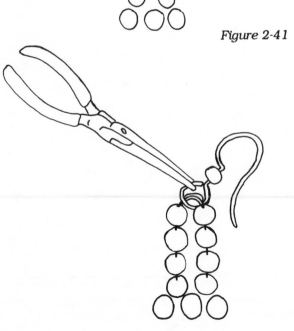

Figure 2-41

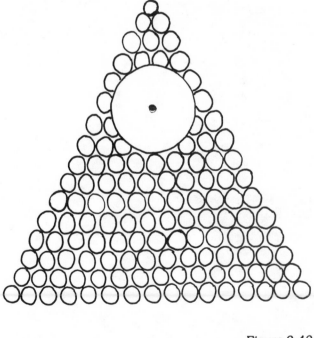

Figure 2-42

11

NOTES

BRICK STITCH DESIGNS

Instructions

The **brick stitch** is used to make flat beaded pieces which are not attached to a material backing. It is the stitch seen in the popular triangular top beaded earrings with a dangling fringe, and it is usually added to a foundation row of seed or bugle beads. A different foundation row is used in each of the three projects in this section. To make the brick stitch appear neat and even, pick out beads of uniform thickness while beading.

To start the **brick stitch**, position the foundation row so that the needle is on the right, with the thread coming out of the top of the last bead. String one bead on the thread and slip the

Figure 3-1

Figure 3-2

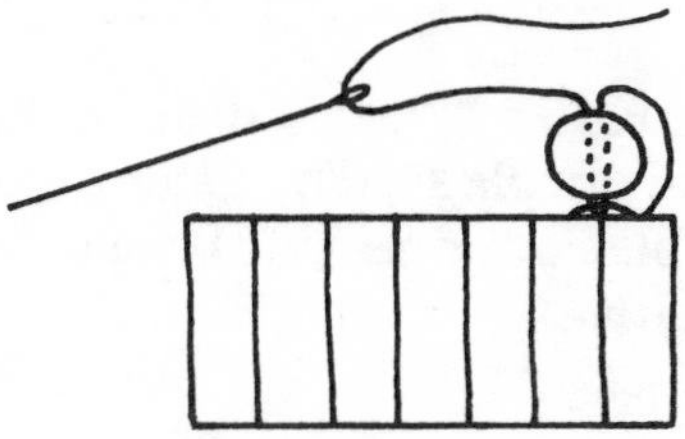

Figure 3-3

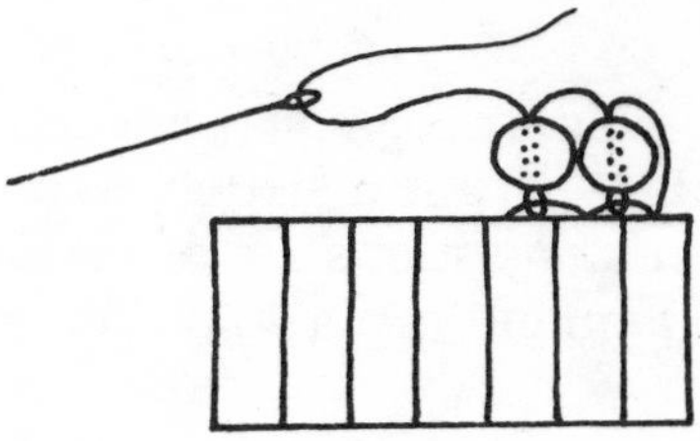

Figure 3-4

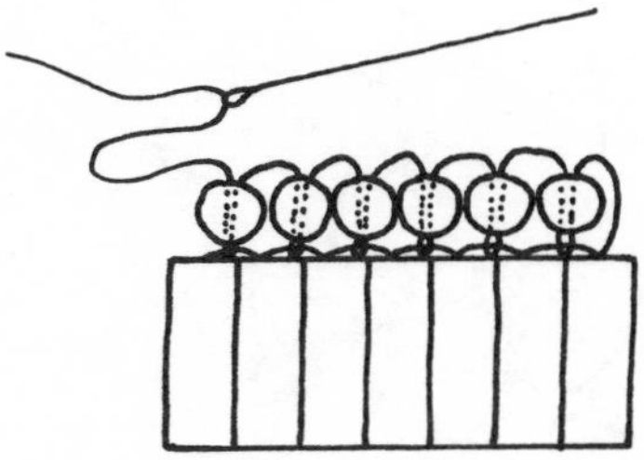

Figure 3-5

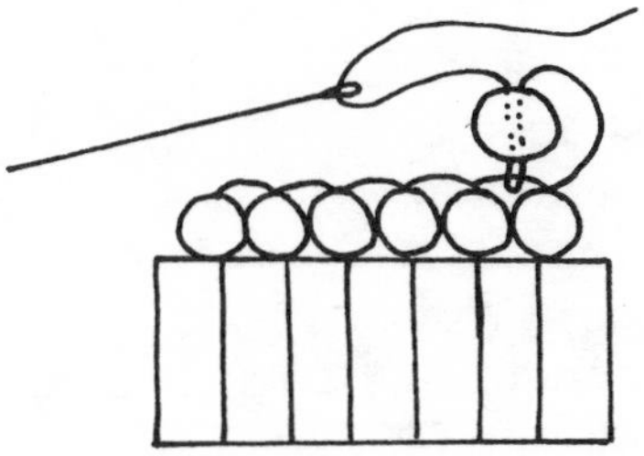

Figure 3-6

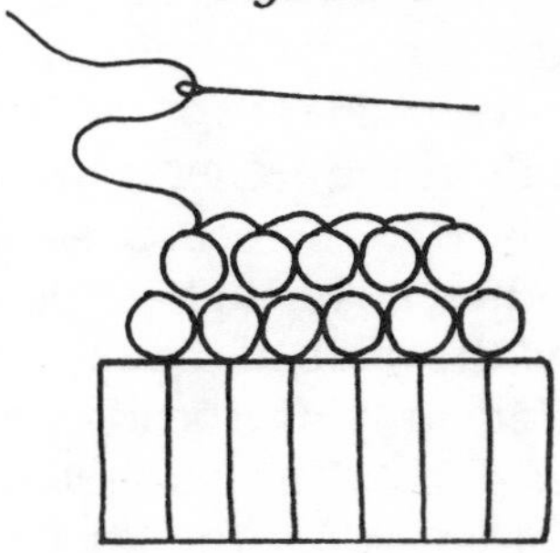

Figure 3-7

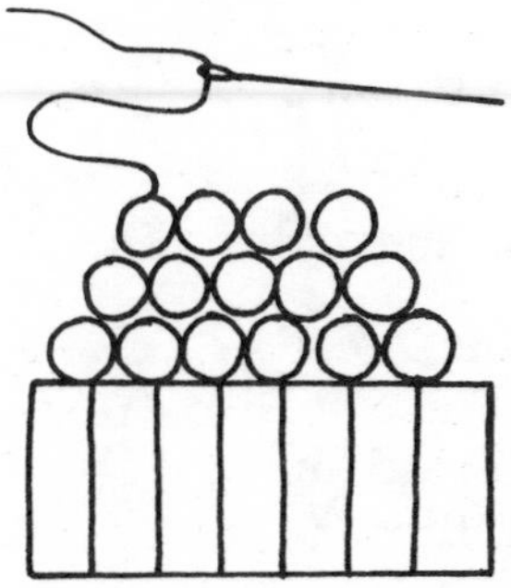

needle under the top thread between the last two beads in the foundation row (Figure 3-1). Pull the thread snug, then bring the needle and thread back up through the new bead (Figure 3-2). The new bead should sit on top of and between the first two beads in the foundation row.

Add a second bead to the thread, slip the needle under the thread between the next two beads in the foundation row, pull the thread snug, and bring the needle and thread back up through the new bead (Figure 3-3).

Continue adding new beads to this row in the same manner; there is one less bead in this row than in the foundation row (Figure 3-4). When the row is completed, turn the work around so that the needle is on the right again and use the same technique to add the next row (Figure 3-5). The number of beads in each row decreases by one as the triangle begins to take shape (Figures 3-6 and 3-7).

Ara's Creation
Brick Stitch Diamonds

Materials Required

Nymo Thread - Size B
Beading Needles - Size 12
Seed Beads - Size 11/°
French Ear Hooks

This design was created by my daughter Ara and utilizes the brick stitch, a staple for beaded earrings. These instructions use pink and purple seed beads, but any color combination can be used. Other suggestions are black and silver, black and red, or brown and gold. The color pattern within the diamond can also be altered; be creative.

Foundation Row

Begin this earring by threading a needle and making a loop knot with two pink beads of uniform size (Figure 4-1a). This knot is described in detail in the General Instructions. Work the knot close to the beads, so that they sit next to each other, before tightening. Tighten the knot by pulling the ends of the thread gently in opposite directions until the beads are snugly side by side (Figure 4-1b). The beads should not be on top of each other. Coat the knot with clear fingernail polish.

Turn the beads so that the knot is on the bottom and string another pink bead on the thread. Pull it next to the other two and attach it by taking the needle and thread down through the second bead (Figure 4-2), then up through the new (third) bead again (Figure 4-3).

String a fourth pink bead on the thread and use the same method to sew it to the third bead. That is, take the needle and thread up through the third bead, then back down through

through the new bead (Figure 3-3).

Figure 4-1a

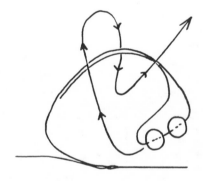

Figure 4-1b

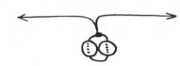

Figure 4-2

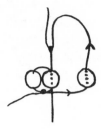

Figure 4-3

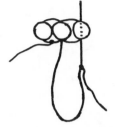

Figure 4-4

Figure 4-5

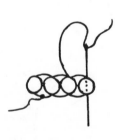

to weave the thread up and down through several beads on this end of the row (Figure 4-6). This will prevent the knot from coming apart. Remove the second needle and clip off any remaining thread on this end.

Beading the Top Half

To start the first brick stitch row, position the beadwork so that the needle is on the right with the thread coming out of the top of the last bead. String one pink bead on the thread, then

Figure 4-6

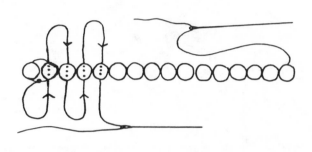

Figure 4-7   *Figure 4-8*

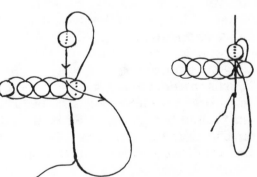

Figure 4-9

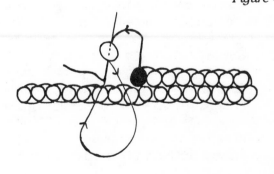

the new (fourth) bead (Figures 4-4 and 4-5).

Continue adding single pink beads and sewing them together in this manner, until the row is sixteen beads in length. Be sure the beads remain side by side. This is the center and widest part of the earring and is called the foundation row.

Finish the foundation row by securing the short piece of thread left at the beginning. Thread a second needle on this piece of thread and use it

Figure 4-10

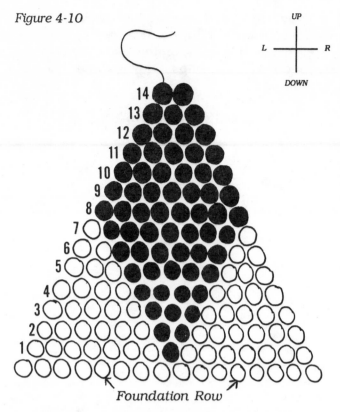

UP
L ─┼─ R
DOWN

14
13
12
11
10
9
8
7
6
5
4
3
2
1

↑ *Foundation Row* ↑

slip the needle under the top thread between the last two beads in the foundation row (Figure 4-7). Pull it down snug, then bring the needle and thread back up through the new bead (Figure 4-8).

Add six more pink beads to this row using the brick stitch described above and in the instructions for Brick Stitch Designs. The eighth bead added should be purple (Figure 4-9). Add seven more pink beads to this first brick stitch row for a total of fifteen beads.

Turn the work around so that the needle is on the right and use the same technique to brick stitch six pink beads, two purple beads, and six more pink beads in the second row. There should be a total of fourteen beads in this row. Turn the work around so that the needle is again on the right.

Continue adding rows in the same manner, using the following beading sequence (Figure 4-10):

Row 3:	5 pink, 3 purple, 5 pink;
Row 4:	4 pink, 4 purple, 4 pink;
Row 5:	3 pink, 5 purple, 3 pink;
Row 6:	2 pink, 6 purple, 2 pink;
Row 7:	1 pink 7 purple, 1 pink;
Row 8:	8 purple;

Rows 9 through 14 are all purple, with one

less bead in each row until there are only two beads in the last (14th) row.

If the earring will be glued to an earring post with a pad, add a final row of one purple bead to the top of the diamond. Skip to the directions for beading the bottom half of the earring.

If ear hooks or an earring post with a drop ring will be used, do not turn the beadwork around after completing the 14th row. Add the attachment loop as described in the next section.

Attachment Loop

Choose six purple beads with large holes as the thread will pass through them three times. String these on the thread after the last brick stitch row has been added.

Take the needle and thread down through the second or right side bead in the top row (row

Figure 4-11

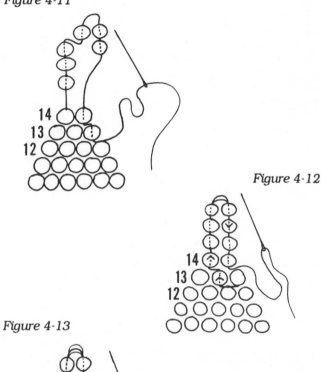

14
13
12

Figure 4-12

Figure 4-13

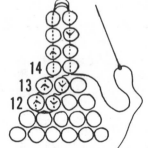

14
13
12

16

14). Continue down through the bead below it (the third bead in row 13). Pull the thread down snug (Figure 4-11).

Bring the needle over and up through the center bead of this row (the 13th) and then through the first bead of the top row (on the left side) . Go through the six loop beads again (Figure 4-12).

Now take the thread down again; go through the second bead in the top row, the middle bead of the next row down (row 13), and continue down through the second bead in row 12. Weave the thread over and up through the first bead in the 12th row. Continue up through the (left) end of rows 13 and 14, and then through the six beads of the loop again (Figure 4-13).

Beading the Bottom Half

To position the thread for beading the bottom half of the earring, weave the thread down

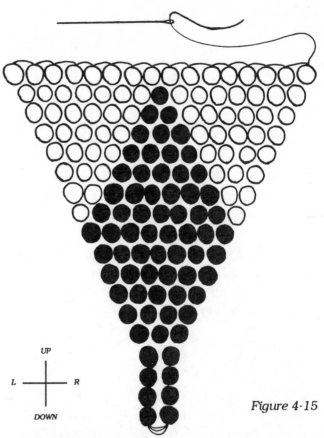

Figure 4-15

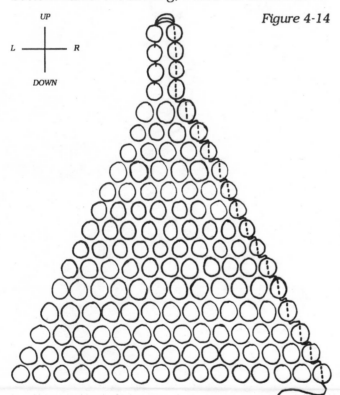

Figure 4-14

the work (Figure 4-15).

Use the same brick stitch technique as was used for the top half of the earring. The bottom half of the earring consists of rows of pink beads. Each row contains one less bead than the preceding row. The last row (the 15th) consists of a single pink bead (Figure 4-16).

Turn the earring right side up. Anchor the end of the thread by weaving it back up into the body of the earring (Figure 4-17). Be sure and weave the thread through several beads from different rows. Remove the needle and clip off any excess thread.

Finishing Touches

A coat of clear fingernail polish may be added to the earring to increase its durability and secure the thread ends. This will also make the earring stiff, an effect which some people do not like. Coating this earring is a matter of personal preference.

To coat the earring, place it on a level surface, making sure that the earring lays flat and has the proper shape. Adjust the bead positions by hand if necessary. Apply the polish

through the end beads on the right side of the beadwork (Figure 4-14). The thread should come out through the bottom of the last bead in the foundation row.

Turn the work upside down so that the loop is on the bottom and the needle and thread are coming out of the top bead at the far right of

Figure 4-16

Figure 4-17

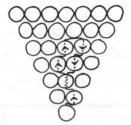

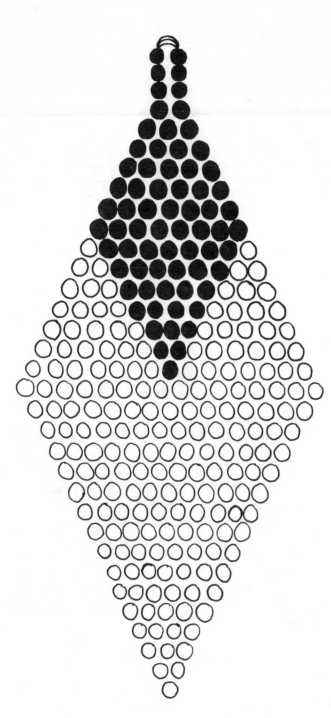

to one side and allow it to dry completely, then turn the earring over and coat the other side.

When the earring is completely dry, mount it on a French ear hook or earring post with drop ring (Figure 4-18) as described in the General Instructions.

The earring is now complete. Make a second earring to match the first and ENJOY!

Figure 4-18

ARA'S CREATION
Brick Stitch Diamonds

Versatile Triangles with Rondelles

Materials Required

Nymo Thread - Size B
Beading Needles - Size 12
Seed Beads - Size 11/°
14 Bugle Beads - Size 3
14 Austrian Crystal Rondelles - 5 mm
French Ear Hooks

This is a variation on a very popular style of beaded earrings, featuring a brick stitch triangular top and dangle fringes. The loop dangles on this design allow it to be made very quickly and when silver rocaille beads are used, it is a very versatile earring. This earring can also be made in other solid colors for easy coordination with any wardrobe.

Foundation Row

Begin this earring by choosing seven bugle beads of uniform length for the foundation row. String two of them on the thread, and tie them together with a loop knot (Figure 5-1; also see General Instructions). Pull the two loose ends of the thread gently in opposite directions to tighten the knot (Figure 5-2). This should draw the two beads snugly together, side by side.

Turn the beads so that the knot is on the top and string a third bugle bead on the thread.

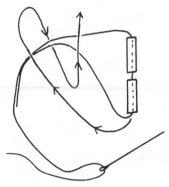

Figure 5-1

Figure 5-2

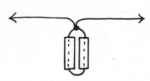

Run the needle and thread up and through the second bugle bead and then down through the new (third) bead again (Figure 5-3). Pull the third bead close and parallel to the first two. The thread should come out of the bottom of the third bugle bead. String on a 4th bugle bead and sew it to the third by coming down through the third bead (Figure 5-4) and then back up through the new (fourth) bead.

Continue to add bugle beads to the foundation row in the same manner until the row is seven beads in length. Stitch the seventh bead to the sixth an extra time for added strength (Figure 5-5).

Complete the foundation row by threading a second needle on the short end of the thread left at the beginning. Weave the needle and thread up and down through several of the bugle beads to anchor it (Figure 5-6). Remove the second needle and cut off any excess thread on this end.

Beading the Earring Body

Place the work so that the needle is on the right, with the thread coming out of the top of the last bugle bead. Brick stitch the triangular body of the earring with five rows of seed beads, starting the first row on the right side of the foundation row (Figures 5-7 & 5-8). This technique is described in the Instructions for Brick Stitch Designs and was used in the Brick Stitch Diamonds project.

Turn the work after each row so that the

Figure 5-3

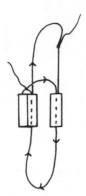

Figure 5-4

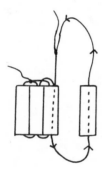

Figure 5-5

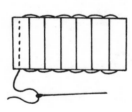

Figure 5-6

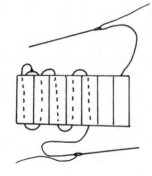

Figure 5-7

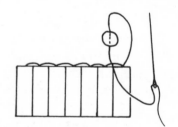

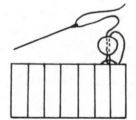

Figure 5-8

20

needle is on the right to start the next row. The fifth row of seed beads should contain two beads (Figure 5-9).

If a French ear hook or earring post with drop ring will be used, leave the needle on the left side of the earring upon completing this row and follow the directions for adding the attachment

Figure 5-9

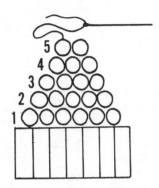

loop.

If the earring will be glued to an earring post with a pad, add a sixth row, consisting of a single bead, at the top of the triangle. Skip to the directions for adding the dangles.

Attachment Loop

Start the attachment loop by choosing six seed beads which are uniform in size and which have large holes. String these on the thread. Run the needle and thread down through the second or right hand bead in the top row. Continue down through the end bead (on the right) in the next row down. Then go over and up through the middle bead of this row (row 4). Continue up through the first or left bead in the top row (Figure 5-10).

Bring the needle through the six loop beads again, then take it down through the right bead of the top row. Continue down through the

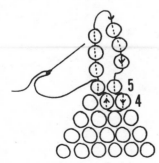

Figure 5-10

Figure 5-11

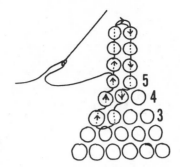

middle beads in the next two rows (rows 3 & 4). Then bring the needle over and up through the bead on the left end of this row (row 4). Continue up through the beads on the left end of the two top rows (Figure 5-11). Go through the six loop beads a third time.

Dangles

To position the thread to add the dangles, work the thread down through the end beads in each row on the right side of the beadwork. Come

Figure 5-12

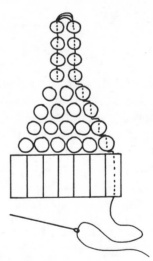

out through the bottom of the end bugle bead on the right side (Figure 5-12).

While making these dangles, remember to pay attention to the thickness of the beads. A string of thick beads will be longer than a string of thin beads and the dangles on opposite sides of the earring must be the same lengths.

To add the first dangle, string 10 seed beads, one crystal rondelle and 10 more seed beads on the thread coming out of the bottom of the end (seventh) bugle bead. Bring the needle

21

Figure 5-13

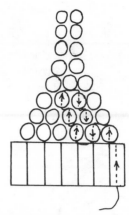

Figure 5-16

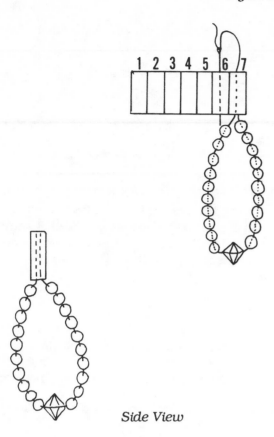

Side View

Figure 5-14

back up through this same bugle bead (Figure 5-13). Adjust the tension in the dangle as described in the General Instructions. Let the top seed beads rest in front and in back of the bugle beads as they naturally tend to do (Figure 5-14).

Run the needle and thread down through the next (sixth) bugle bead. String on 17 seed beads, one crystal rondelle and 17 seed beads. Take the needle back up through the sixth bugle bead (Figure 5-15).

The third dangle consists of 24 seed beads, one crystal rondelle and 24 seed beads and is attached to the fifth bugle bead. The fourth dangle is the longest and is attached to the middle bugle bead. Use 31 seed beads, one crystal rondelle and 31 seed beads.

The fifth dangle is the same as the third one, the sixth dangle repeats the second one and, of course, the seventh dangle is the same as the first. This last dangle should be attached to the first bugle bead on the left end of the foundation row.

Anchor the thread in the body of the earring by weaving the thread back and forth through several beads in different rows (Figure 5-16).

Finishing Touches

Lay the earring flat on a clean surface. Shape the top by hand, pushing the beads into

Figure 5-17

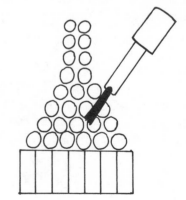

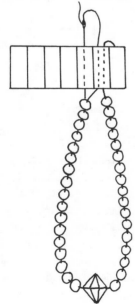

Figure 5-15

their proper places. Coat the upper part of the earring, including the row of bugle beads, with clear fingernail polish (Figure 5-17). Be careful not to get any fingernail polish on the dangles. It is not necessary to coat both sides of this earring.

The fingernail polish stiffens the earring top, forcing it to keep its shape. The earring will last longer because the beads do not move and fray the thread.

When the earring is completely dry, mount it on a French ear hook or other finding as described in the General Instructions. Make a second earring and these are ready to wear!

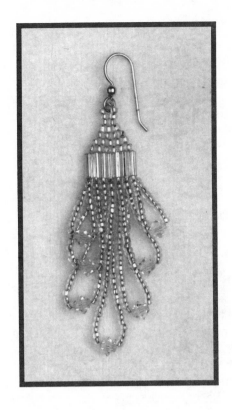

*Versatile Triangles
with Rondelles*

Multicolored Quill and Stone Bead Earrings

Materials Required
Nymo Thread - Size B
Beading Needles - Size 12
Cut Seed Beads - Size 9/°
22 Round Stone Beads - 5 mm
22 Porcupine Quills
Sharp Knife
French Ear Hooks

These earrings are real eye catchers - very large and elaborate. They are made with a brick stitched triangular top and long dangles which incorporate the beautiful, natural look of porcupine quills and semiprecious stone beads.

The colors used in the instructions are gold, black, purple, turquoise blue and cobalt blue, and these colors are particularly suited to use with garnet stone beads. Many other wonderful and unique earrings can be made with this same pattern by simply changing the colors used. One example would be to use cream, copper, gold and dark brown seed beads with tiger eye stones in the dangles.

The instructions for these earrings rely heavily on techniques described in the Brick Stitch Instructions and used in the first two projects. It would be a good idea to read these sections before beginning work on this project.

23

Quill Preparation

Before beading these earrings, prepare the porcupine quills as described in the General Instructions. Cut the quills so that the pieces are one of the following lengths: One inch for long earrings; 3/4 inch for medium length earrings; or 1/2 inch for short earrings.

Foundation Row

The foundation row forms the center of this earring. This row requires beads which are very uniform in size, so choose them carefully. Pick out four gold beads, four black beads, eight purple beads, four turquoise blue beads and two cobalt blue beads for this row.

Thread the needle and string two gold beads on the thread. Tie them together, on top of one another, with a loose loop knot. Put the needle inside both gold beads (Figure 6-1) to keep them lined up and gently tighten the knot by pulling the two threads in opposite directions. The knot should be drawn snugly against the beads and positioned near the bottom (Figure 6-2).

Pull the needle up through the two gold beads, turn the beads so that the knot is on the

Figure 6-5

Figure 6-6

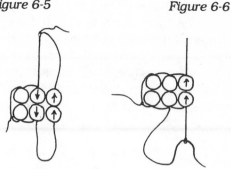

left, and string on two black beads (Figure 6-3).

Bring the needle up through the two gold beads again, then back down through the black ones. Pull the new beads snug against and parallel to the first two (Figure 6-4).

String on two purple beads and run the needle down through the black beads, then up through the purple beads (Figure 6-5 and 6-6). Pull the new beads snugly against the others.

Continue adding beads to the foundation row, using the same technique as above. The color sequence for the rest of the row is: two purple, two turquoise; two cobalt; two turquoise; two purple; two purple; two black; and two gold beads (Figure 6-7). Stitch the last set of beads (gold) to the black ones twice for added strength.

Complete the foundation row by weaving

Figure 6-1

Figure 6-2

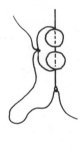

Figure 6-7

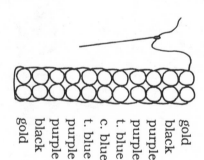

gold
black
purple
purple
t. blue
c. blue
t. blue
purple
purple
black
gold

Figure 6-3

Figure 6-4

the short thread at the beginning of the work up and down through several of the beads in this row. Pull the thread tight, remove the second needle and clip off any excess thread.

Beading the Earring Body

Brick stitch the triangular top of the earring with nine rows of seed beads, following the

24

color-keyed diagram in Figure 6-8. This stitch is described in the Instructions for Brick Stitch Designs and the Brick Stitch Diamonds project. The color sequence for each row is as follows with g = gold, b = black, p = purple, and c = cobalt blue:

Row 1:   g, b, p, p, c, c, p, p, b, g;
Row 2:   g, b, p, c, p, c, p, b, g;
Row 3:   g, b, c, p, p, c, b, g;
Row 4:   g, b, p, p, p, b, g;
Row 5:   g, b, p, p, b, g;
Row 6:   g, b, p, b, g;
Row 7:   g, b, b, g;
Row 8:   g, b, g;
Row 9:   g, g.

If a French ear hook or earring pad with drop ring will be used, do not turn the work around after the last row. The needle and thread should be positioned on the left side of the top

which have big holes. String these on the thread coming out of the top row.

Weave the thread down through the top two rows of brick stitch, then back up to the loop beads as described in the previous two projects.

Go through the loop beads again and down into the body of the earring. Weave the thread down through the top three rows, then back up to the loop beads once again. Pass through the loop beads a third time to assure a strong top on the earring.

Dangles

Work the thread down through the end beads in each row on the right side of the earring. Come out through the bottom of the foundation row on the right side, in position to sew on the

Figure 6-8

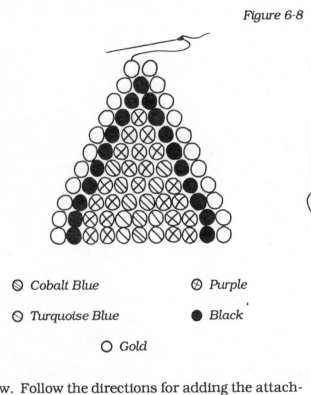

⊘ Cobalt Blue   ⊕ Purple

⊙ Turquoise Blue   ● Black

○ Gold

row. Follow the directions for adding the attachment loop.

If an earring post with a pad will be used, add a tenth row, consisting of a single gold bead, to the top of the triangle. Skip to the directions for adding the dangles.

Attachment Loop

Start the attachment loop by picking out six gold beads which are uniform in size and

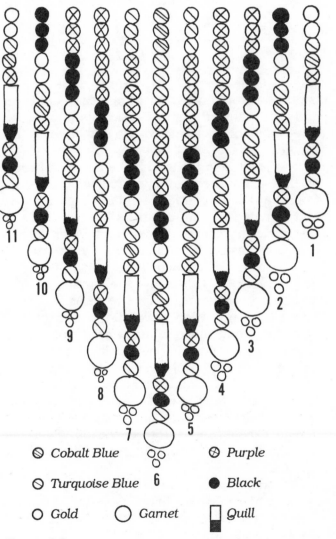

⊘ Cobalt Blue   ⊕ Purple

⊙ Turquoise Blue   ● Black

○ Gold   ◯ Garnet   ▯ Quill

Figure 6-9

dangles. For the first dangle, string the following on the thread: two gold, one turquoise blue, one cobalt blue, and one purple bead, one porcupine quill, one purple, one black, and one turquoise blue bead, one garnet stone bead, and three small gold beads (Figure 6-9).

Starting with the garnet, run the needle

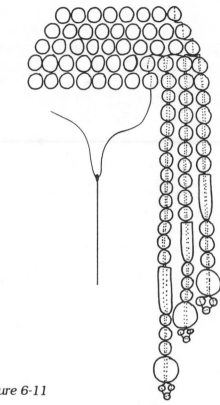

Figure 6-11

Figure 6-10

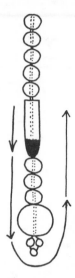

back up through the remaining beads (and the quill) in the strand (Figure 6-10). This gathers the three small beads at the bottom and anchors the thread.

Continue up through the two gold beads on this end of the foundation row (Figure 6-11). Note that the thread for each dangle goes down and then back up through the same two beads in the foundation row. Adjust the tension in the dangle as described in the General Instructions.

Come back down through the next two beads (black) on this end of the foundation row and string on the beads for the second dangle. These are: three black, two gold, one turquoise blue, one cobalt, and one purple bead, one porcupine quill, one purple, one black, and one turquoise blue bead, one garnet stone bead, and three small gold beads (see Figure 6-10).

Again starting with the garnet, bring the needle back up through all the elements of the dangle except the last three beads. Then go through the two black beads in the foundation row again.

Add the remaining dangles in the same manner, attaching one to each set of beads in the foundation row. The composition of the remaining dangles is shown in Figure 6-9.

The beading sequence adds three beads to the top section of each dangle. The first three are purple at the top of the third dangle, then another three purple at the top of the fourth, three turquoise blue beads at the top of the fifth and three cobalt blue beads at the top of the sixth or middle dangle. After this the dangles on the second half of the earring decrease in length, mirroring the dangles on the first half. Thus the seventh dangle is the same as the fifth, the eighth is the same as the fourth and so on.

Choose the size of the beads carefully, so that a uniform taper is maintained between the dangles. If some of the beads are too small, add extra beads to achieve the proper length for each dangle. Since the color combination at the bottom of each dangle is the same, any additions will be less noticeable if they are made in the top portion of the dangle.

When the dangles are completed, anchor the thread by weaving it up into the body of the earring, passing it through several beads in different rows. This procedure is illustrated in the previous project. Remove the needle and clip off any excess thread.

26

Finishing Touches

Lay the earring on a flat, clean surface and press the top triangle into shape, straightening and flattening it. Paint the top part of the earring with clear fingernail polish on both sides, allowing it to dry between sides. Be careful not to get any fingernail polish on the dangles. Allow the earring to dry completely.

When making the mate to this earring, be sure to measure the length of the first one and match the second one to it.

All that remains is to attach the earrings to French ear hooks or earring posts. Use good quality findings to complement the quality of the work.

*Multicolored Quill and Stone
Bead Earrings*

NOTES

PEYOTE DESIGNS

Instructions

The **peyote or barrel stitch** is used to bead around or cover three dimensional objects, and to make "free standing" pieces of round beadwork or beadwork cords. This stitch creates a network pattern of beads and always begins with an even number of beads in the first (foun-

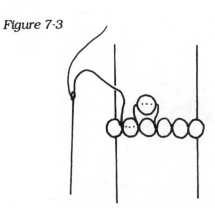

Figure 7-3

Figure 7-1

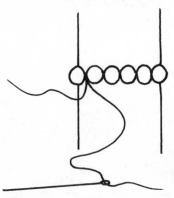

dation) row. Subsequent rows have half as many beads as the foundation row. Each row "nests" in the gaps between beads from previous rows, so that a repeating pattern is established.

Usually, even "free standing" pieces are beaded around a cylindrical object, such as a match or straw, which is removed when the beadwork is finished. The number of beads used in the foundation row depends on the desired size of the piece, but it must be an even number;

choose an object with the right diameter and lay strung beads around it to determine the right number of beads to use.

String the beads for the foundation row on the thread and fasten them together with a loop knot, but do not tighten the knot just yet. Slip the ring of beads this creates on a round object of the right diameter, and then tighten the loop knot (Figure 7-1).

String one bead on the thread. Skip the first bead in the foundation row and put the needle through the second bead (Figure 7-2). Pull the thread snug, setting the new bead in position above the first bead in the foundation row (Figure 7-3).

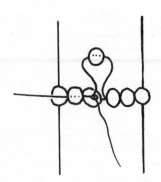

Figure 7-2

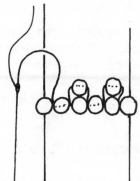

Figure 7-4

29

Add a new bead to the thread, skip the next (third) bead in the foundation row and take the needle and thread down through the fourth bead in the foundation row (Figure 7-4). This creates a small gap between the new beads, into which the next row will fit.

Continue adding new beads and stitching through every other bead in the foundation row until the new row is complete. End by bringing the needle up through the first bead in this new row (Figure 7-5). This is called a **step up**, and it is critical to maintaining the pattern of the stitch. Every row must end with a step up.

In the next row, the thread passes through every bead in the previous row and the new beads fit into the gaps between those beads. New gaps are created and the pattern of the stitch is formed (Figure 7-6).

Figure 7-5   Figure 7-6

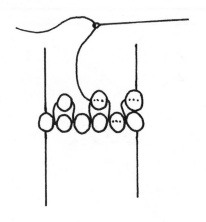
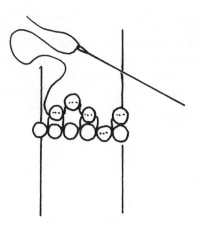

Peyote Barrel Top Earrings

Materials Required

Nymo Thread - Size B
Beading Needles - Size 13
Seed Beads - Size 12/°
12 Bugle Beads - Size 3
12 Austrian Crystal Rondelles - 5 mm
Wooden Match
Ear Wires or Posts

This earring is made with the peyote stitch, which is always started with an even number of beads. The color design in this piece requires that the first number be divisible by four. This beginning number can be varied for larger or smaller earrings, but for this example it will be twelve. Again, any color combination may be used, but black, white, red and blue have been used to demonstrate the design. Also, a quick note on technique: with beads this small, it is easiest to put the beads in shallow jar lids, pick them up with the tip of the needle and slide them onto the thread.

Foundation Row

To start this earring, choose twelve uniform black beads; thin beads (those which are narrower from top to bottom) are needed here so that the foundation row will be the right size. Thread a needle and pick up all twelve black beads. Tie them together with a loop knot, forming a ring of beads, but do not tighten the knot.

Slip the ring of beads, with the knot on the bottom of the ring, on a wooden "kitchen" match with a circumference of about a half inch and a length of at least two inches. Center the ring vertically on the match and tighten the knot by

Figure 8-1

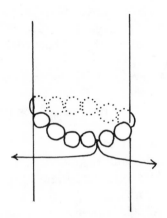

pulling the threads in opposite directions. Make sure the beads are snugly against one another around the match (Figure 8-1).

Put a second needle on the short piece of thread left hanging from the knot and run it through several of the beads again to hide and secure this end (Figure 8-2). Remove the second

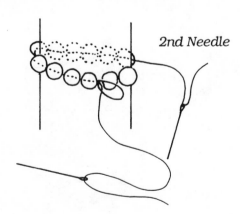

Figure 8-2

needle and cut off any extra thread.

Building the Barrel Top

This project varies from the basic Peyote Design Instructions in that it has a single row,

called the "drop row", below the foundation row. To start, make sure the needle and thread are below the foundation row. Pick up a single black bead. Skip the first bead in the foundation row and put the needle up through the second bead (Figure 8-3). Pull the thread snug so that the new bead rests below the first bead in the foundation row.

Pick up another black bead. Skip the next bead in the foundation row and put the needle up

Figure 8-3

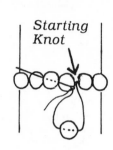

Starting Knot

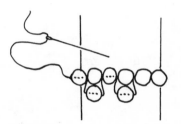

Figure 8-4

through the fourth bead in this row (Figure 8-4). The new bead should rest below the third bead of the foundation row.

Continue adding one black bead below every other bead in the foundation row. The thread will pass through the sixth, eighth, tenth, and 12th beads of the foundation row. There should be six beads in this new row.

End the row by passing the needle and thread through the first bead of the foundation row (Figure 8-5). The thread should emerge above the foundation row. This is very important for positioning the thread to bead above the

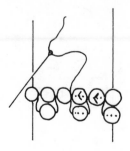

Figure 8-5

foundation row. Every row must end with a positioning stitch such as this, called a "step up". The step up places the thread in the row to which the next bead will be added.

The drop row will eventually be the top of the earring and the earring loop will be attached to it after the body of the earring is beaded. Leave

Figure 8-6

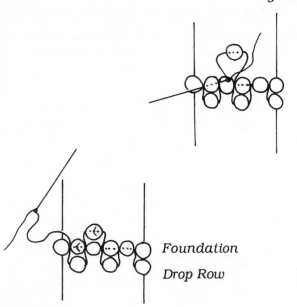

Figure 8-7

it as is for now. The rest of the rows in the barrel top are all added above the foundation row in the manner described in the Peyote Design Instructions.

To begin the first row in the barrel top, pick up one black bead. Put the needle down through the third bead of the foundation row (Figure 8-6). Pull the thread tight, setting the new bead in position over the second bead in the foundation row (Figure 8-7).

Continue all the way around the match in

this fashion, stitching new beads on top of every other bead of the foundation row. Again, there will be six beads in this row.

Finish the row with a step up through the first bead of the *new* row (Figure 8-8). This takes the thread from the foundation row to the first row of the barrel top. Skipping this step will change the pattern of the stitch.

Continue to build the barrel, adding rows of six beads on top of the previous rows. In these rows, the thread passes through every bead in the previous row. Remember to step up into each new row as it is completed. Use the color sequence below and refer to the color-keyed diagram in Figure 8-9 as needed. In the rows with alternating colors, the first bead must be the first color mentioned.

Row 2 : all black beads;
Row 3: all black beads;
Row 4: alternate one black and one white bead;
Row 5: all white beads;
Row 6: alternate one white and one red bead;
Row 7: all red beads;
Row 8: alternate one red and one blue bead;
Row 9: all red beads;
Row 10: alternate one red and one white bead;
Row 11: all white beads;
Row 12: alternate one white and one black bead;
Rows 13 through 16: all black beads.

Figure 8-9

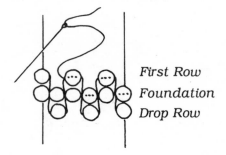

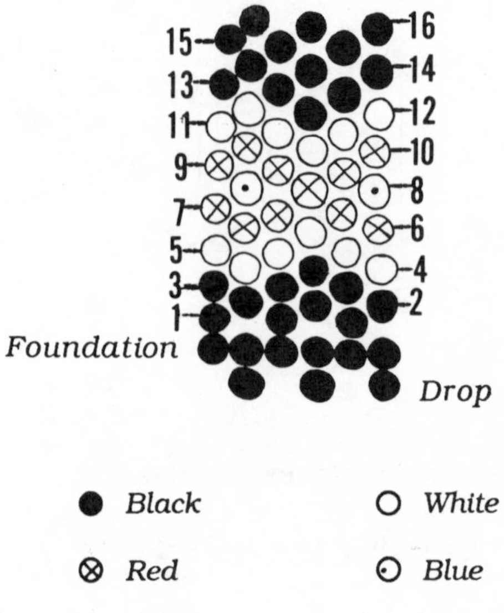

First Row
Foundation
Drop Row

Figure 8-8

Dangles

Leave the beadwork on the wooden match and invert the whole piece so that the last row beaded and the thread are on the bottom. This will make it easier to work on the dangles which are attached to this bottom row (row 16).

To create the first dangle, string four black seed beads, then one each of white, red and blue on the thread coming out of the last row beaded. Add another red bead, one white bead and one blue bugle bead. Now add one bead each of white, red, blue, red, and white. End with four black beads, a 5 mm crystal rondelle, and three small blue beads (Figure 8-10).

Starting with the crystal, run the needle back up through all the dangle beads except the last three. This gathers the three small beads at the bottom and anchors the thread.

Adjust the tension in the dangle as de-

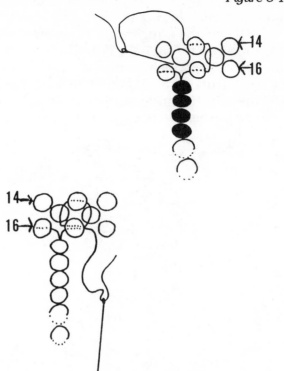

Figure 8-12

Figure 8-13

scribed in the General Instructions. Make sure the tension in the thread is the same coming up the dangle as it was going down.

Run the thread through the next (second) bead in the bottom row (row 16) of the barrel (Figure 8-11). Then circle up through the bead just above this one in row 14 (Figure 8-12), and down through the second bead in row 16 again (Figure 8-13). This step anchors each dangle and keeps them hanging evenly.

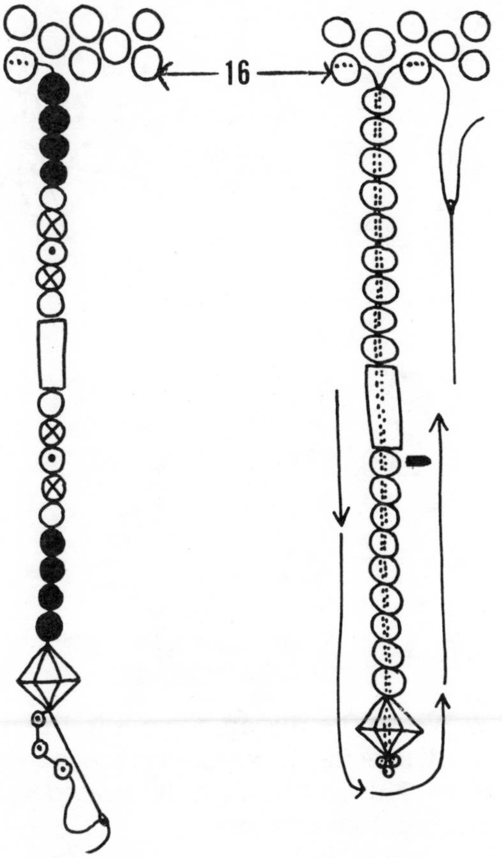

All the dangles on this earring are the same (see Figure 8-10). Add five more dangles around the earring, using the same technique as for the first one. The second dangle hangs between the second and third beads in the bottom row, the third dangle between the third and fourth beads,

Figure 8-10   *Figure 8-11*

← 16 →

Figure 8-14

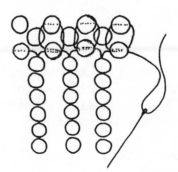

● Black   ○ White

⊗ Red   ◉ Blue

and so on (Figure 8-14). Anchor each dangle through a bead in row 14.

When the dangles are completed, weave the thread up through the beads of the barrel to the drop row, which is now at the top of the earring (Figure 8-15). This positions the thread to add the attachment loop. Pull the match down through the beadwork until the top of the match

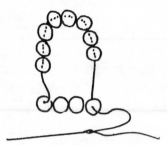

Figure 8-17

Figure 8-15

is just below the level of the drop row.

Attachment Loop

Go around the match through all the beads in the drop row and pull the thread snug, folding the beads over the top of the match (Figure 8-16). Repeat this step, going through all the beads in the drop row a second time, and pull the thread snug once again.

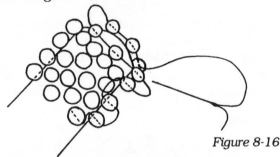

Figure 8-16

Choose eight black beads of uniform size, with large holes for the loop. String them on the thread. Arch the thread over the top of the barrel and, counting the bead from which the thread emerges as one, run the needle through the fourth bead, on the opposite side of the barrel top (Figure 8-17).

Thread the needle back through the beads of the loop (Figure 8-18) and into the bead in the drop row where the loop started. Run the needle through beads one through four in the drop row, around the top of the barrel (Figure 8-19). Finally, go back through the loop beads a third time (Figure 8-20).

Figure 8-18

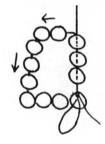

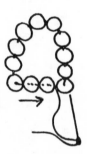

Figure 8-19

Weave the thread down into the barrel to anchor it, passing through several beads in different rows. This technique is illustrated in the first two Brick Stitch projects.

Finishing Touches

Coat the barrel with clear fingernail polish,

Figure 8-20

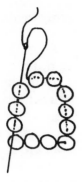

being careful not to get any on the dangles. Turn the match to keep the beads from sticking to it while the earring is drying, but do not remove the match until the polish is dry. Stick the end of the match in the top of a spool of thread to keep the wet nail polish from touching anything as it dries. Add earring hooks or posts and this earring is ready to wear.

*Peyote Barrel
Top Earrings*

Beaded Crystal Cap
Necklace or Earrings

Materials Required

Nymo Thread - Size A
Beading Needles - Size 15
Seed Beads - Size 14/°
Quartz or Amethyst Crystals
Epoxy Putty
20 Gauge Silver Wire - 2 inches

Beading is a good way to mount crystals for ornamental use. Many people find that crystals channel the energy flows of their bodies in positive ways. Metal, which can interfere with those energy flows, need not touch a crystal when a beaded cap is applied. Beaded crystals can be mounted as necklaces or as earrings. This design is done with the peyote stitch. If this stitch is not familiar, read the Peyote Design Instructions before beginning this project.

The colors used in the instructions are transparent rose and opaque white, but any combination which complements the colors in the crystal can be used. Do not hesitate to elaborate on the color design or carry it further up the stone, especially if the crystal is a large one. If a different color pattern is desired, the design used for the Peyote Barrel Top earrings can also be used with attractive results.

Crystal Preparation

To prepare the crystal a smooth, beadable surface must be added, along with a means of attaching the crystal to earring or necklace findings. Begin by making a wire attachment loop. A sterling silver Shepherds Hook ear wire can be straightened to provide the silver wire. Take the silver wire and bend a small hook in one end (1/8 to 1/4 inch long, depending on the size of the crystal). Leave enough wire on the other end to wrap back around itself, then bend the wire over the round point of a pair of needle-nosed pliers. Make a loop big enough for a necklace chain. Wrap the end of the wire around the straight

Figure 9-1   section below the loop (Figure 9-1).

Now look closely at the crystal and visualize how it should look when it is finished. Suppose the raw crystal looks like the one in Figure 9-2. The jagged top will not allow a cap of beads to sit on it smoothly, but this is the end which should be covered. It is simple to reshape the crystal with gray or white epoxy putty, which sets rock hard and provides a point of attachment.

Estimate the amount of putty needed to add a smooth dome to the top of the crystal. There must be enough putty to imbed the attachment wire to the bottom of the necklace loop. Following the directions on the putty package, cut off equal amounts of each of the two colors. Mix them together thoroughly until the two colors blend into one and the putty is warm to the touch.

Figure 9-2

Put this blob of putty on top of the crystal and shape it into a dome with smooth sides and enough depth to hold the wire firmly when the putty is set.

Immediately imbed the hook end of the wire in the putty, pushing it straight down into the middle of the dome, with the loop sticking up. Leave about 1/16 inch between the bottom of the

loop and the top of the putty cap so that the beads can be worked right up to the wire (Figure 9-3). Let the putty dry until it is hard, usually 24 hours.

Figure 9-3

Once the putty is dry, a "lip" to anchor the cap of beads must be built around the crystal. Take about three feet of nymo thread (more or less, depending on the thickness of the crystal) and tie a loose loop knot in one end. Slip the loop created by the knot around the crystal and place it just below the putty. Pull the thread ends to tighten the loop around the crystal.

Tightly wrap the long thread end around the crystal, on top of the first loop, 12 to 15 times. Build a lip which is thick enough to keep the cap of beads from pulling over it, but do not make it so thick that it will cause a bulge in the finished beadwork (Figure 9-4). Tie the two ends of the thread together with a square knot and clip off any extra thread. Coat the thread lip with clear fingernail polish or super glue and let it dry.

Figure 9-4

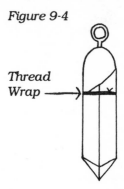

Thread Wrap →

Foundation Row

The beads for this project are very small, so it is important to choose beads with holes large enough for the needle and two strands of thread to pass through easily. Thread a size 15 needle and string on enough rose beads to make a smooth circle around the crystal, just below the thread lip. Remember that for the peyote stitch there must an even number of beads in this row.

Tie the beads together in a circle with a loose loop knot. Work the knot close to the beads, but do not tighten it. Slip the ring of beads over the tip of the crystal (Figure 9-5) and slide it up to just below the lip of thread. Tighten the ring of

Figure 9-5

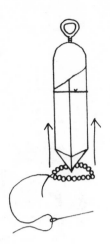

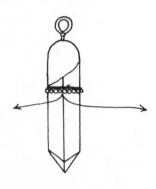

Figure 9-6

beads on the crystal by pulling the thread ends (Figure 9-6).

Hide the short end of the thread by putting on a second needle and running it through half of the beads in the foundation row. Remove the needle and cut off any excess thread.

Beaded Cap

Use the peyote stitch and add a row of rose beads above the foundation row. There should be

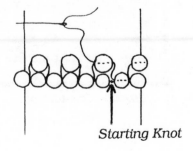

Starting Knot

Figure 9-7

half as many beads in this row as in the foundation row. Don't forget the step up at the end of the row (Figure 9-7).

Start the next row with a rose bead and alternate rose and white beads around the crystal (Figure 9-8).

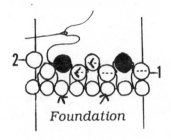

Foundation

● White

○ Rose

Figure 9-8

Begin the third row above the foundation row with a white bead and alternate white and rose beads to start a pattern of diagonal lines around the crystal (Figure 9-9).

It must be stated here that these instructions are only meant as an example of how to do the work. It is impossible to give a bead by bead pattern here, since every crystal has a different

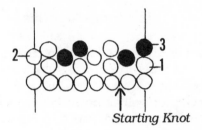

Starting Knot

Figure 9-9

size and shape and all beads vary in thickness. Thus, although Figure 9-9 shows the third row starting with a white bead, this may not always be correct. Look at the color pattern being created to determine which color bead should be added next. By following the directions and *feeling* the right way while laying the beads in place, much can be gained in terms of beading skill.

The fourth and fifth rows also alternate rose and white beads to continue the diagonal design (Figure 9-10). The fourth row should theoretically start with a rose bead and the fifth with a white bead.

Figure 9-10

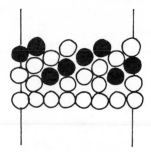

Figure 9-11

Bead the rest of the cap with transparent rose beads and the peyote stitch. On larger crystals, it may look better to alternate more rows, or if the crystal is a very small one, fewer alternating rows may be called for in building the beadwork toward the top of the dome.

When the dome begins getting smaller at the top, start picking out thinner beads to stitch into the rows. As the beadwork becomes even tighter, start skipping beads where necessary to pull the work together around the top. Do this by passing the thread through two beads in the previous row without adding a bead between them. After skipping a bead, it may be necessary to use two beads in one stitch in the next row to fill the hole created. Play it by ear. The main thing is to *just keep going*. Fill in the entire top, snuggling the top beads close to the wire (Figure 9-11).

Finishing Touches

Weave the thread back down through about ten beads in different rows to secure the end. This is most effective if the thread is woven sideways within rows as well as down between rows. Cut off any excess thread and dab clear fingernail polish on the area where the thread was cut.

Put a chain through the loop on the crystal to make a necklace, or put a Shepherds hook on the looped wire for use as an earring.

Beaded Crystal Cap

CABOCHON DESIGNS

Instructions

The same basic steps are used to create all the bead and cabochon jewelry pieces in this section. Read these instructions carefully before attempting any of these projects. It might also be a good idea to review the Materials section for information on the additional supplies needed for these projects.

Getting Started

Use a six to ten inch embroidery hoop and enough pellon or interfacing to fill the hoop. Generally a square which is two inches larger than the hoop will suffice. Put the pellon in the embroidery hoop. Stretch the material tight and

Figure 10-1

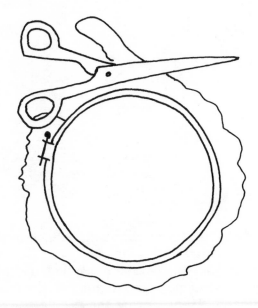

secure the hoop firmly around it. Use scissors to cut off any excess pellon that sticks out around the bottom of the hoop (Figure 10-1).

Next glue the cabochons to the pellon. Smear a thin, even layer of glue on the flat back of each cabochon and firmly press the stones on the fabric. Leave enough room around each stone

to allow for the beadwork as specified in each project (Figure 10-2). The more space left around the stones, the easier they will be to work around. Remove any excess glue with a fingernail or knife. Allow the glue to dry for at least an hour. Draw any pattern guidelines which are needed on the pellon at this time. These are specified in each project.

Figure 10-2

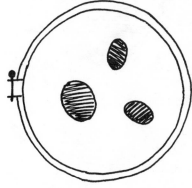

Beading the Rosette

Thread a beading needle and put an anchor knot in the long end of the thread. This knot is described in the General Instructions. Trim off any excess thread and coat the knot with clear fingernail polish. Bring the threaded needle up through the pellon, close to the stone, at the point specified for each pattern (point A in Figure 10-3).

Add the first string of beads to the thread. The number and colors of these beads will be specified for each pattern; generally each string will be about a fourth of the beads needed to

Figure 10-3

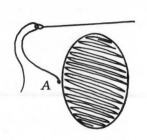

Figure 10-6

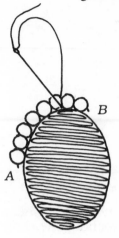

Figure 10-4

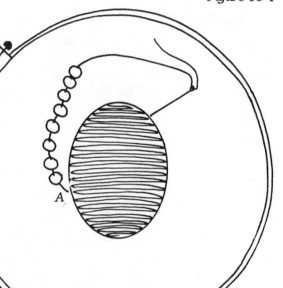

Figure 10-7

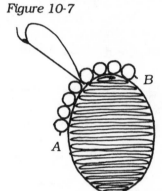

Figure 10-8

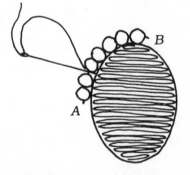

Figure 10-5

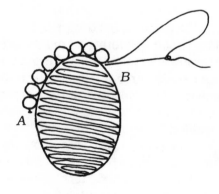

complete the first row around the cabochon. Lay the beads around the stone in a clockwise direction (Figure 10-4). Take the needle back down through the pellon at point B and pull the thread snug (Figure 10-5). Bring the needle back up through the pellon between the second and third beads from point B, go over the thread connecting the two beads, and back down through the pellon (Figure 10-6). Sew the rest of the beads in this string to the pellon, taking stitches over the thread between every other bead (Figures 10-7 & 10-8).

This method of sewing beads to fabric is called the **overlaid** or **applique stitch**. The stitch used in this book is a variation of the running stitch commonly used in beading. It can also be used to outline and fill the interior of a design drawn on pellon or other material.

When using the overlaid stitch around cabochons, the direction of the stitch is important. If the string of beads is part of an interior row, bring the needle up on the outside of the thread connecting the beads, and stitch over it towards the stone. This is shown in the above Figures. However, if the string of beads is part of the outside or last row of beads around the cabochon, the direction of these stitches is reversed. Bring the needle up through the pellon on the inside of the connecting thread. Take the needle over the connecting thread, and angle it

Figure 10-10

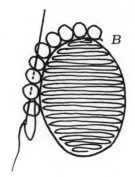

Figure 10-11

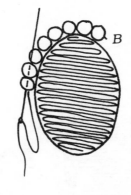

Figure 10-9

Figure 10-12

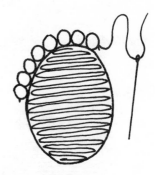

back under the thread, towards the cabochon, as it reenters the pellon (Figure 10-9). This tucks the threads under the beads as much as possible and protects them from being cut when the beadwork is removed from the pellon. The reversed stitch can not be used on all the rows because it causes too much bunching.

When the beads in the first string have been stitched to the pellon, run the needle and thread back through the beads, from the point at which the stitching ends to point B. Note that the thread will go through all but the first bead if there are an odd number in the string (Figure 10-10) or through all the beads if there are an even number (Figure 10-11). Because of the curve around the stone, this step must be done through

two or three beads at a time. The thread is now in position to continue stitching the first row of beads around the stone (Figure 10-12).

Pick up the next string of beads, lay them around the next portion of the stone, and stitch them to the pellon with an overlaid stitch, in the same manner as the first string of beads (Figures 10-13 & 10-14). Run the needle back through the beads, ready to add the next string (Figure 10-15). Continue in this manner around the stone until the last string of beads is added for this row.

Connect the last string of beads to the beginning of the row by running the needle through the first bead (Figure 10-16). Take the needle down through the pellon on the far side of this

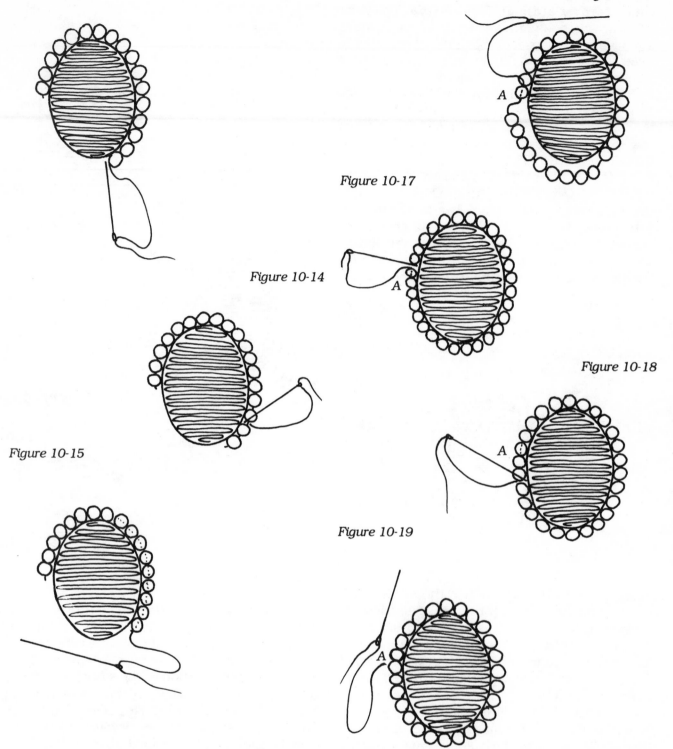

Figure 10-13

Figure 10-16

Figure 10-17

Figure 10-14

Figure 10-18

Figure 10-15

Figure 10-19

bead (Figure 10-17), then stitch the last string of beads to the pellon in the same manner as before. Take the first stitch between the second and third beads from the end of the line just added (Figure 10-18).

Run the needle back through the beads to the starting point (A). Take a small sideways stitch in the pellon; emerge half a bead width outside the first row, ready to add the next row around the cabochon (Figure 10-19).

42

Add the rest of the rows around the cabochon in the same manner as the first. Follow the bead pattern specified in each project. Reverse the direction of the stitching on the last row and secure the end of the thread with a finishing knot on the back of the pellon. This knot is described in the General Instructions. Coat the knot with clear fingernail polish.

Bead all the cabochons on the pellon before proceeding further with any individual piece.

Mounting Earrings

Cabochon earrings are mounted on earring pads with 7/16 inch posts before the beadwork is removed from the embroidery hoop. Smear a thin even layer of glue on the flat side of the earring pad (Figure 10-20). Stick the glued side of the pad to the back of the pellon (Figure 10-21). Use the stitches on the back of the pellon as a guide for placing the pads. On round cabochons, center the pad on the back; on oval cabochons, place the pad a little above center, so the earring will hang straighter when it is worn

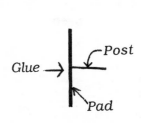

Figure 10-20

Figure 10-21

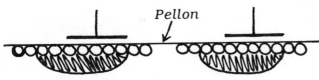

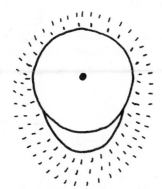

Figure 10-22

(Figure 10-22). Allow the glue to dry for at least an hour before continuing.

Remove the pellon from the embroidery hoop and cut the earrings out of the pellon. Leave about 1/8 inch of pellon around each of the rosettes to prevent the beadwork from getting glue on it when the leather backing is added.

Mounting Other Jewelry

If a brooch, barrette, necklace or bolo tie is being made, remove the pellon from the embroidery hoop as soon as the beadwork is completed. Trim the pellon close to the beadwork, being careful not to cut any threads. Lay the trimmed beadwork on a piece of thin plastic and trace around the beadwork with a marking pen. Remove the beadwork from the plastic and draw another outline about 1/16 inch inside the first line (Figure 10-23). Cut out the plastic disc on the inside line. Making the plastic smaller than the beadwork keeps it hidden inside the leather backing and it is easier to stitch the beadwork to the leather because the needle doesn't have to go through the plastic. The plastic stiffens the rosette, improving its appearance and increasing

Figure 10-23

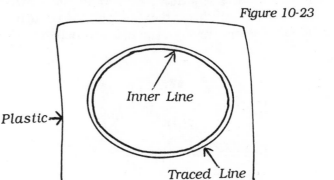

its longevity.

Glue the plastic disc to the pellon side of the beadwork, using a thin layer of glue on the plastic. Center the disc so that a little bit of pellon can be seen all the way around the plastic.

Leather Backing

All of the cabochon jewelry is backed with leather; choose colors which match or complement the beadwork. The leather hides the stitching, earring pads and plastic, and makes the jewelry more comfortable to wear. It also provides a surface for attaching bar pins, barrette clasps

Figure 10-24

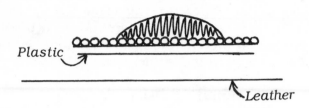

and other findings which go on the back of jewelry pieces. Leather backed pieces of jewelry can be kept clean with a soft toothbrush and a little dish soap.

Spread the leather, rough side up, on top of a thick piece of styrofoam (6" x 6" x 1"). Set the beadwork pieces on the leather to determine where they should be glued. Make sure they will not overlap. Mark the position of earring posts with a pen.

Use a small Glover's needle to punch a hole through the leather for the earring posts. Draw a small circle around each hole to make it easier to locate.

Smear the backs of the beadwork, including the steel earring pads and plastic discs, with glue. Push the glued pieces onto the leather (Figure 10-24). For earrings, insert the posts into the styrofoam through the holes punched in the

Figure 10-25

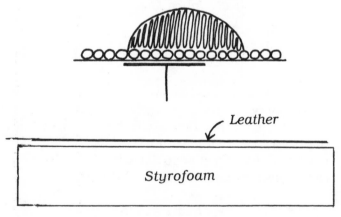

leather and press the glue against the leather (Figure 10-25).

Remove the leather from the styrofoam and press the leather to the beadwork again. Seal it tight around the edges and around the posts. Clean off the earring posts if necessary. Allow the

Figure 10-26

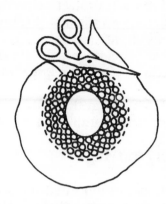

glue to dry for several hours.

Trim the excess leather from around each of the pieces. Cut close to the beads, but be careful not to cut any threads (Figure 10-26).

Thread a short beading needle and tie an anchor knot in one end. Coat the knot with clear fingernail polish. Starting at the bottom of the beadwork, push the needle between the the two outermost rows of beads, from the beadwork side to the leather side (Figure 10-27). Pull the knot down between the rows of beads to hide it. Use the needle nosed pliers to pull the needle through

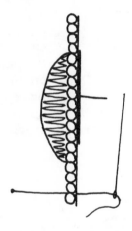

Figure 10-27

the leather if needed.

Stitch the leather to the beadwork all the way around the outer edge with a running stitch. In this context, the **running stitch** is a sewing stitch which simply involves pushing the needle through the beadwork, from front to back and then from back to front, all the way around the edge of the beadwork. Take large stitches on the front of the beadwork, where the stitches do not show and the thread is protected by the beads. Take small stitches on the back where the stitches show and are not protected (Figure 10-28). If the piece will be edged, end with the thread on the

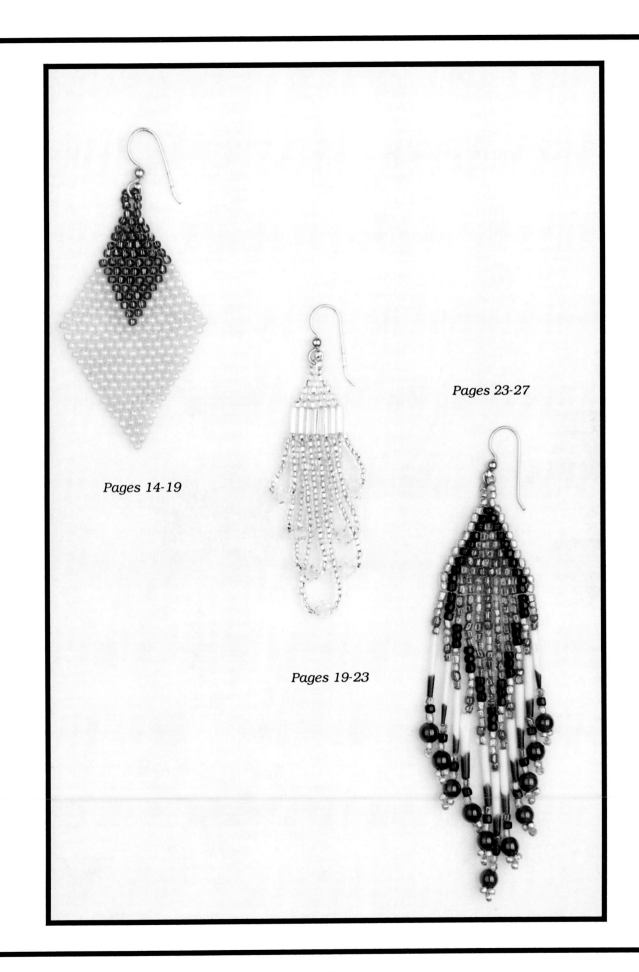

Pages 14-19

Pages 23-27

Pages 19-23

C1

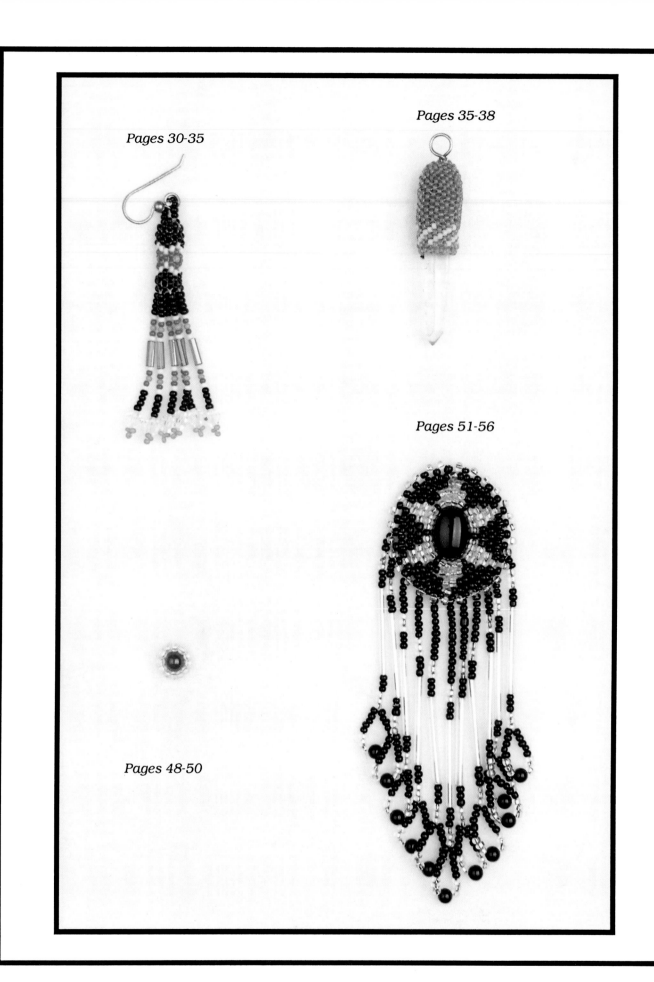

Pages 30-35

Pages 35-38

Pages 51-56

Pages 48-50

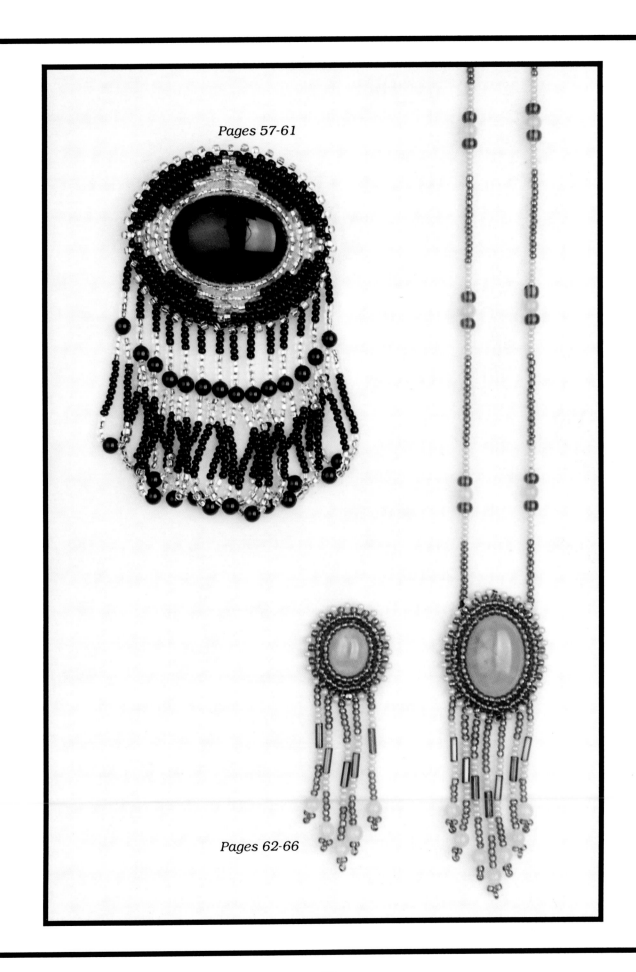

Pages 57-61

Pages 62-66

Pages 67-74

Pages 75-82

C4

Figure 10-28

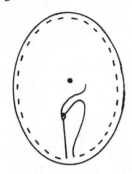

beaded side of the jewelry, at the bottom. If not, end on the back and secure the thread with a finishing knot.

Edging the Beadwork

Most of the cabochon projects in this book are edged with a three bead **loop edging stitch** and use contrasting colors. It is important to choose beads which are as uniform in size as possible for this stitch. Begin with the needle and thread on the beaded side of the work, just inside the outer row. Run the needle through one of the outer beads (Figure 10-29) and rotate the beadwork so

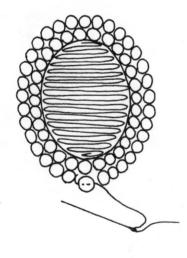

Figure 10-29

that the needle and thread are at the top. The edging stitches are easier to make from this position. String three beads on the thread, one of the first color, one of the contrasting color, and another of the first color. Working counterclockwise, skip two beads in the outer row of the beadwork, and run the needle under the thread connecting the second and third beads from the starting point (Figure 10-30). Bring the needle back up through the third edging bead (Figure 10-31). Pull the thread snug, squeezing the

Figure 10-30

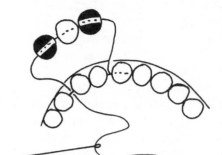

Figure 10-31

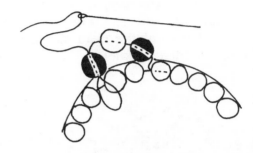

middle edging bead to the top of the other two.

Add two more beads to the thread; one of each color, with the contrasting color first. Skip two beads in the outer row of the beadwork and

Figure 10-32

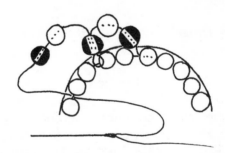

Figure 10-33

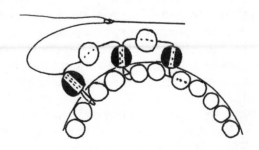

run the needle under the connecting thread between the second and third beads from the previous stitch (Figure 10-32). Bring the thread back up through the second bead just added (Figure 10-33). Pull the thread snug, squeezing the first bead to the top.

Continue adding two beads at a time and stitching them to the outer row all the way around the beadwork. Remember that an even appearance is more important than skipping exactly two beads between each stitch (see Beading Tips). To connect the ends of the edging, string on one bead of the contrasting color and run the needle down through the first edging bead stitched to the piece (Figure 10-34). Push the needle through to the back of the beadwork, between the two outer rows of beads. At this point the beadwork can be completed with a finishing knot on the back, or a

Figure 10-35

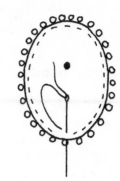

Figure 10-34

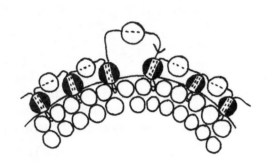

dangling fringe may be added without knotting the thread.

Dangles

The most common method of adding dangles is to start in the center (at the bottom) and work to one side, then return to the center and work to the opposite side. Which side is done first is a matter of personal preference. Dangles can also be started on one side and worked around the bottom to the opposite side. The best method will be specified for each project.

For cabochon jewelry, all dangle stitches must be taken into or through the leather only. Do Not go through to the front of the beadwork with these stitches.

With the thread on the back of the piece, take a small vertical stitch to the edge of the leather (Figure 10-35). Add the beads for the first dangle and then bring the thread back up through

the beads specified for that dangle. Take a small vertical stitch in the leather, directly above the dangle (Figure 10-36 a & b). Adjust the tension in the dangle (see General Instructions), then take an angled stitch which emerges at the edge of the leather, one eighth inch to one side of the previous dangle (Figure 10-37).

This is the location of the next dangle, but before it is added, a **securing stitch** is necessary to prevent the thread from pulling out of the leather and to isolate each dangle from the effects

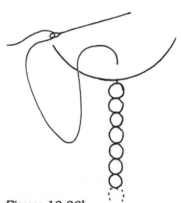

Figure 10-36a

Figure 10-36b

of neighboring dangles if they are pulled or broken. This is a small vertical stitch, beginning 1/16 of an inch above the edge and emerging through the same hole as the previous angled stitch (Figure 10-38). Repeat this vertical stitch, using the same holes, to complete the securing stitch (Figure 10-39). String the beads for the next dangle on the thread and continue in this

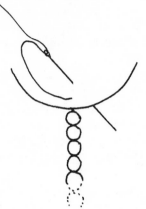

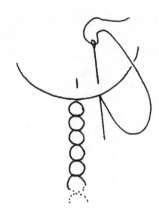

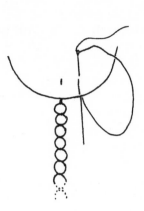

manner until all the dangles have been added to the first side.

After the tension is adjusted in the last dangle, put the needle back into the leather about 1/8 inch above the dangle stitch and run it out to the side of the rosette (Figure 10-40). Circle the needle back through the holes just made in the leather and pull the thread through until a small

Figure 10-40

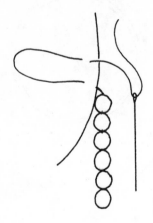

loop remains (Figure 10-41). Tie a finishing knot, using this loop as the starting loop. Clip the thread close to the knot and coat the knot with fingernail polish.

If the dangles were started in the middle of the cabochon, thread the needle again and tie an anchor knot in one end. Push the needle between the two outer rows of beadwork, from front to back, about 1/8 inch to the other side of the middle dangle. Pull the knot down between the beads to hide it. Take a small vertical stitch to the edge of the leather, positioning the thread to add the first dangle on this side (Figure 10-42). Continue in the same manner as the first side until all the dangles have been added, then secure the end of the thread with a finishing knot in the same manner as above.

Remember to match the taper of the dangles on both sides of each earring and to make sure that the dangles on each earring in a pair are the same length. Techniques for doing this are described in the General Instructions.

Figure 10-41

Figure 10-42

Small Cabochon Button Earrings

Materials Required

Nymo Thread - Size B
Long Beading Needles - Size 12
Short Beading Needles - Size 12
Glover's Needle
2 Round Matching Cabochons - 4 mm
Seed Beads - Size 11/°
2 Earring Pads with Posts & Ear Nuts - 4 mm
Leather - 1" x 1"

These earrings are small, simple and elegant. They are a good project for beginners and they require only 22-26 beads. Be sure and buy extras (at least 40) so that size and shade can be matched. Also, read the Cabochon Design Instructions before starting this project.

Many variations of this simple design can be made. The pair made for this book have garnets surrounded by crystal iris beads, but the possibilities are as endless as one's imagination. Other possibilities are black onyx cabochons with silver or red beads; jade cabochons with gold beads; and carnelian cabochons with red beads. Dangles can also be added. Make more than one pair.

Getting Started

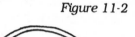

Put a piece of pellon in an embroidery hoop. Stretch the cloth tight and cut off any excess pellon sticking out around the bottom of the hoop (Figure 11-1).

Figure 11-2

Figure 11-1

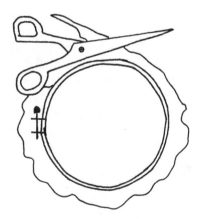

Figure 11-3

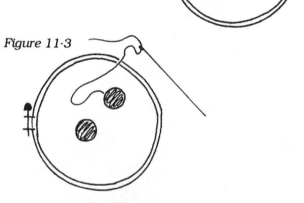

Beading the Buttons

Glue both stone cabochons firmly to the pellon, leaving at least 3/4 of an inch around each stone. More space around the stones makes the work easier. Immediately remove any excess glue from the stones and pellon. Allow the glue to dry for at least one hour (Figure 11-2).

Thread about 18 inches of nymo thread on a long beading needle and tie an anchor knot in one end. Bring the needle and thread up through the pellon as close to the first stone as possible, leaving the knot on the under side of the cloth (Figure 11-3).

String 12 seed beads on the thread and lay the strung beads around the stone. The beads should lay smoothly and evenly around the stone. If they are too tight, remove one and use only eleven beads. If they are loose, with gaps between them, add a 13th bead (Figure 11-4).

With the beads around the stone, put the needle down through the pellon one bead past the start of the row. Stay right next to the stone

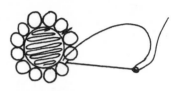
Figure 11-4

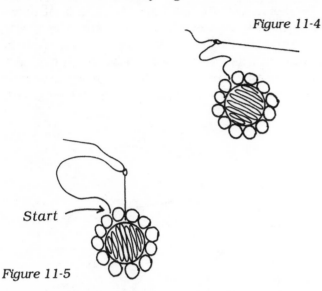
Figure 11-5

(Figure 11-5). Place a thumb on top of the stone to help hold the beads in place and tighten the thread until the beads are comfortably snug around the stone. If the beads begin to bunch up around the stone, the thread is too tight.

Bring the needle back up through the pellon between the 3rd and 4th beads from the beginning of the row, next to the stone (Figure 11-6). Go over the thread connecting these beads, then put the needle back down through the

Figure 11-6

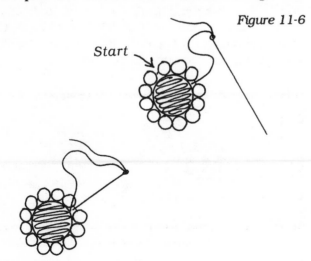

Figure 11-7

pellon, angling it back towards the stone (Figure 11-7). This is the reverse overlaid stitch described in the Cabochon Designs Instructions. Since there is only one row of beads, it is important that the thread be protected by tucking it under the beads.

Continue stitching around the string of

Figure 11-8

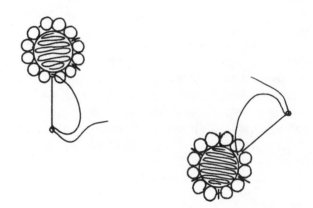

Figure 11-9

Figure 11-10

beads in this manner, taking a stitch between every other bead (Figures 11-8 and 11-9). End with a second stitch between the third and fourth beads (Figure 11-10) and the needle on the pellon side of the work. Tie a finishing knot to secure the thread. Bead around the matching stone in the same fashion as the first one to create the second button.

Mounting The Buttons

Glue the 4 mm earring pads (with posts) to the back of the beadwork. Center the pads in the middle of the buttons, using the stitches on the back as a guide. Allow the glue to dry for at least an hour (Figure 11-11).

Cut the beadwork out of the pellon, leaving about 1/8 inch of cloth around each piece to shield the beads from the glue during the follow-

Figure 11-11

Figure 11-12

ing steps (Figure 11-12).

Now add a leather backing to the earrings. First, spread the small piece of leather, rough side up, over a thick piece of styrofoam. Use a Glover's needle to punch two holes in the leather which are 1/2 inch apart, making sure that the beaded cabochons will sit entirely on the leather when the posts are pushed through the holes. Mark the holes with a pen.

Smear the leather liberally with glue. Im-

Figure 11-13

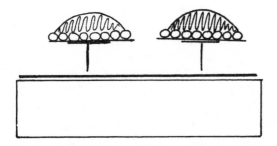

mediately push the posts (glued to the backs of the buttons) through the holes in the leather and into the styrofoam. Press the beadwork down firmly on the glue smeared leather (Figure 11-13).

Remove the leather and beadwork from the styrofoam. Cut the leather into two pieces, with one earring on each piece. Clean off the posts and press the leather and pellon together again, sealing them together around the edges and around the posts. Allow the glue to dry for several hours.

After the glue is dry, trim the excess leather and pellon from around the buttons. Cut close to the beads, but be careful not to cut any threads.

Thread a short beading needle with about one foot of nymo thread. Make a loop knot in one end of the thread. Put the needle down between the beads and the stone, passing through both the pellon and the leather. Pull the knot down and hide it between the stone and the beads (Figure 11-14). Needle-nosed pliers may come in handy at this point, as it can be tough to pull a small needle through leather. Simply push the needle through both layers, then grab the tip with

Figure 11-14

Figure 11-15

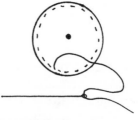

Figure 11-16

the pliers and pull it through.

Stitch the leather to the beadwork all the way around the button, using a running stitch through both layers. Take longer stitches on the beaded side to hide the thread and shorter stitches on the leather side (Figure 11-15). End with the needle and thread on the leather side of the button (Figure 11-16) and tie a small finishing knot to secure the end of the thread.

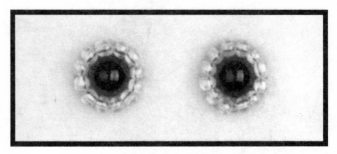

*Small Cabochon
Button Earrings*

Star Rosette Earrings

Materials Required

Nymo Thread - Size B
Long Beading Needles - Size 12
Short Beading Needles - Size 12
Glover's Needle
2 Cabochons - 10 mm x 14 mm
Seed Beads - Size 11/° & Size 10/°
22 Bugle Beads - 1"
22 Round Stone Beads - 4 or 5 mm
Earring Pads with Posts & Ear Nuts - 14 mm
Leather - 3" x 6"

Onyx cabochons with black and silver beads make these earrings very dramatic and despite their size, they are wonderfully comfortable to wear. The pattern can be adapted to many beautiful creations by varying the bead colors and the kind of stones. Other possible combinations are black and red, black and violet, black and gold, or even black and blue. The black can also be left out in exchange for white or purple.

The instructions for these earrings assume familiarity with the Cabochon Design Instructions. Read this section before attempting this project.

Getting Started

Put a piece of pellon in an embroidery hoop, stretching the cloth tight. Cut off any excess pellon sticking out around the bottom of the hoop.

Firmly glue both onyx cabochons to the pellon, leaving at least 3/4 of an inch of open space around each stone. Again, the more space left, the easier the work will be. The position of the

Figure 12-1

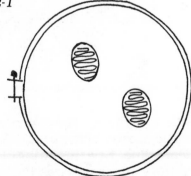

stones is not critical, however for the purposes of giving directions it will be assumed that the long dimension of each oval is vertical (Figure 12-1).

With a pencil and ruler, draw guidelines on the pellon which extend at least 1/2 inch beyond the stones as shown in Figure 12-2. These lines

will be used to keep the beadwork straight, so make straight, accurately centered lines. First draw vertical lines at the top and bottom center of each stone. Then draw dotted horizontal lines which are centered on either side of the stones.

Figure 12-2

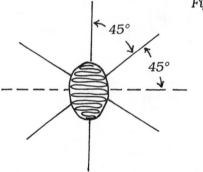

Divide each of the four sections just created around each stone in half. These lines should be at 45° angles to the original lines.

Beading the Rosettes

Use size 11/° seed beads in the rosettes to achieve finer detail in the pattern. Thread a long beading needle and tie an anchor knot in one end of the thread. Clip off any excess thread and coat the knot with clear fingernail polish.

To begin beading, bring the needle up through the pellon just to the left of the top

Figure 12-3

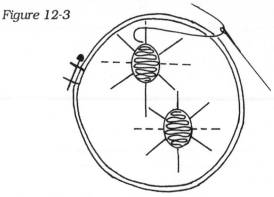

vertical guideline, next to the first stone (Figure 12-3).

String 3 silver, 1 black, 4 silver, and 1 black seed bead on the thread. Lay this string of beads clockwise around the stone. The silver beads must straddle the solid guidelines, with one to the left and two to the right of the top line and two on each side of the angled line. The last black bead must sit on the dotted center line (Figure 12-4). Choose beads of the appropriate width (thick or thin) to fit this pattern, substituting if necessary. When the right size beads are on the thread, push the needle down through the pellon, just below the dotted center line.

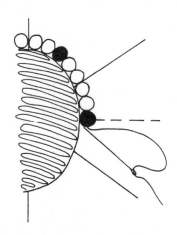

Figure 12-4

Stitch the first string of beads to the pellon with a regular overlaid stitch. Use the placement of the stitches to adjust the positions of the beads as necessary, ensuring that they are correctly placed relative to the guidelines. Run the needle back through all the beads except the first one.

Pick up 4 silver, 1 black, and 2 silver beads on the thread. Lay this string of beads around the

stone so that there are two silver beads on either side of the bottom angled guideline. The last silver bead should lie just to the right of the bottom vertical guideline (Figure 12-5). Substitute beads of different widths as needed to fit the pattern.

Push the needle down through the pellon on the bottom vertical guideline. Stitch these beads to the pellon with an overlaid stitch and run the needle back through all but the first bead, positioning the thread to string on more beads.

String 2 silver, 1 black, 4 silver and 1 black bead on the thread. Figure 12-5 shows the

Figure 12-5

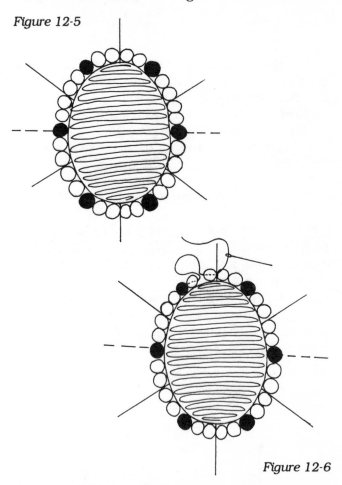

Figure 12-6

correct position of these beads relative to the guidelines. The second black bead must sit on the dotted center line. Sew this string of beads to the pellon in the same manner as the first two.

To complete this row, add 4 silver, 1 black and 1 silver bead to the thread. Position the beads as shown in Figure 12-5 and run the thread through the first silver bead at the top of the stone (Figure 12-6). Stitch the beads down to the pellon as before, then run the needle and thread back through the beads just added.

To position the needle for the second row, take a small sideways stitch in the pellon. Put the needle down through the pellon, next to the stone, on the top guideline. Bring it back up just above the beads of the first row, to the left of the top vertical guideline (Figure 12-7).

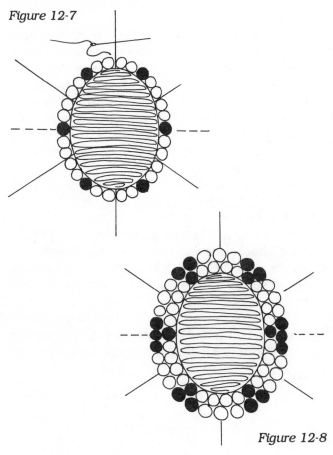

Figure 12-7

Figure 12-8

Start the second row by stringing 2 silver, 2 black, 3 silver and 2 black seed beads on the thread. Lay this string of beads clockwise around the stone and check their positions against Figure 12-8. Note that the first silver bead should be on the top guideline, the middle bead of the three silver beads should be on top of the angled guideline and the last black bead should be on top of the dotted horizontal guideline. Stitch these beads to the pellon.

Continue adding beads to the second row and stitching them to the pellon in the same fashion as the previous beads. Note that the middle bead in each series of three silver beads sits on top of a solid guideline. Refer to Figure 12-8 for the correct position of these beads. The second string of beads in this row should be 1

black, 3 silver, 2 black and 3 silver beads.

For the third string of beads add 2 black, 3 silver, and 2 black beads to the thread. The fourth and final series of beads consists of 1 black, 3 silver, 2 black, and 1 silver bead. End this row with a small stitch to position the thread for the third row. The thread should emerge from the pellon so that the first bead in the new row will be to the left of the top guideline.

Add the third row as shown in Figure 12-9. Break the row into four strings of beads with 11 beads in the first three strings and 9 beads in the fourth. The silver beads in this row need to be on either side of the solid guidelines. As the beading moves further from the stone, it may become more difficult to find beads of the correct width to match the pattern of the design. If necessary, add or delete black beads to ensure

Figure 12-9

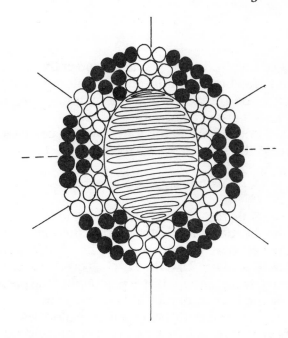

that the silver beads are correctly placed. Maintaining the pattern is more important than using the exact number of beads provided in these instructions.

Stitch the fourth row to the pellon in the pattern shown in Figure 12-10. Since this is the outside row of the rosette, use a reverse overlaid stitch. Break the row into four strings of beads which are 15, 13, 12 and 13 beads in length. The silver beads in this row must sit on top of the solid guidelines. Make sure the stitches in this row are

Figure 12-10

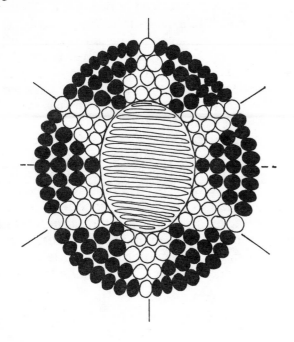

Figure 12-11

ally with glue, covering an area at least as big as both pieces of beadwork.

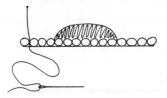

tucked well under the beads to protect them later when the beadwork is cut out of the pellon. Secure the thread with a finishing knot on the back side of the beadwork.

Repeat the same four rows of beadwork around the second onyx cabochon.

Mounting the Rosettes

Glue the 14 mm earring pads to the backs of the beaded onyx cabochons, slightly above center so that the earring will hang straighter when it is worn. Use the stitches on the back of the beadwork as a guide for positioning the pads. Allow the glue to dry for at least an hour.

Cut the beadwork out of the pellon, leaving approximately 1/8 inch extra pellon around each rosette to keep the glue off the beads during the following steps.

Next, the rosettes must be backed with leather. Black leather makes an attractive backing for this color combination. Spread the leather, rough side up, over the piece of styrofoam. Punch two holes in the leather, about three inches apart, with a Glover's needle. Make sure there is room for both rosettes to sit entirely on the leather when the posts are pushed through the holes. Mark the holes with a pen.

Smear the leather around the holes liber-

Immediately push the earring posts through the holes and into the styrofoam. Firmly press the rosettes on the glue smeared leather.

Remove the leather and beadwork from the styrofoam. Cut the leather into two pieces, with one earring on each piece. Clean off the posts and press the leather and pellon together again, sealing the edges tightly. Allow the glue to dry for several hours.

Cut the beadwork out of the leather. Trim the pellon and leather close to the beads, but be careful not to cut any threads.

Thread a short beading needle and tie an anchor knot in one end of the thread. Starting on the front of the beadwork at the bottom, push the needle through the rosette, between the outer two rows of beadwork (Figure 12-11).

Stitch the leather to the beadwork all the way around both rosettes, using a running stitch through both the leather and pellon. Take small

Figure 12-12

stitches on the back and hide longer ones between the bead rows on the front. Use needle nosed pliers to pull the needle through the leather if needed.

End with the needle and thread on the bottom of the beaded side of the rosette. Run the needle through the bottom bead of the outermost row of beads (the silver one on the bottom guideline; Figure 12-12) and switch back to a long beading needle on the thread. Finish the earrings one at a time from this point on.

Edging the Rosettes

Use size 10/° beads in the edging to give a fuller look. Choose approximately 20 seed beads of each color (silver and black) which are uniform in thickness for the edging around each rosette.

Use a loop edging stitch around the outside of the rosettes. Start by stringing 1 black, 1 silver, and 1 black seed bead on the thread (Figure 12-13). Skip two beads in the outer row of the beadwork and run the needle under the

Figure 12-13

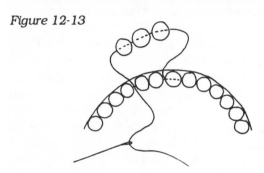

thread connecting the 2nd and 3rd beads from the starting point. Pull the thread snug, squeezing the middle edging bead to the top of the other two beads. Take the needle back through the last black bead of the three just added (Figure 12-14). Add 1 silver and 1 black bead to the thread and

Figure 12-14

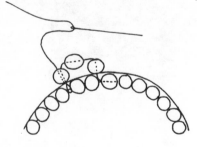

continue edging all the way around the rosette. Finish the edging by adding a single silver bead and running the thread down through the first black edging bead.

Push the needle through to the back of the rosette between the two outer rows. Take a small vertical stitch to the edge of the leather, so that the thread is at the exact center of the bottom of the beadwork. This positions the thread to string on the dangle fringes.

The Dangles

Use size 10/° seed beads, the inch long bugle beads and black onyx round beads to make the dangles. For the first dangle, string the following beads on the thread coming out the

Figure 12-15

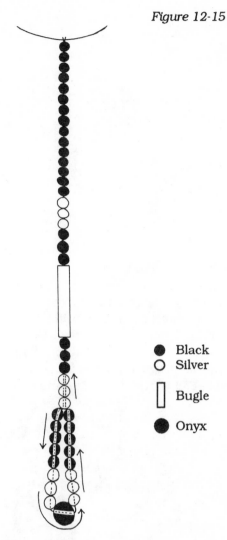

● Black
○ Silver
▯ Bugle
● Onyx

bottom of the rosette: 15 black, 3 silver and 3 black seed beads; 1 inch long silver bugle bead; 3 black, 3 silver, 5 black and 3 silver seed beads; 1 round black onyx bead; 3 silver and 5 black seed beads. Bring the needle back up to the third silver seed bead below the bugle bead, and run the needle and thread up through this bead and the rest of the beads above it in the dangle (Figure 12-15).

At the top of this string of beads, put the needle back in to the leather at the bottom of the rosette. Emerge from the leather approximately 1/16 inch above the entrance of the needle. Adjust the tension in the dangle so that the beads swing freely (see General Instructions). Put the needle back in to the leather, close to the point of emergence, and angle it to come out on the edge of the leather, 1/8 inch to one side of the first dangle (Figure 12-16). Make a vertical securing stitch in the leather before adding the beads for

Figure 12-16

the next dangle.

Add five more dangles to this side of the earring, using the same technique as for the first one. Each dangle should be 1/8" from the last. Omit 3 or 4 black beads from the top of each successive strand, making sure that the bottom of the dangles hang with a uniform taper (Figure 12-17). When the last dangle on the first side is

done, secure the thread with a finishing knot as described in the Cabochon Design Instructions.

Thread the long beading needle again and push the needle between the two outer rows of beadwork, from front to back, 1/8 inch to the other side of the first (middle) dangle. Pull the knot down between the rows of beadwork to hide it. Take the needle down through the leather to the edge of the rosette, positioning the thread to start a new dangle on the second half of the rosette (see Figure 12-17).

Add five dangles on the second side of the earring, using the same procedure and bead sequences as the first side. Make sure the taper of the bottom of the dangles is the same on both sides. Secure the thread with a finishing knot.

Add the edging and dangles to the second earring. Make sure that the lengths of the dangles on the two earrings match.

Color the threads on the back of the rosettes with a black marking pen to hide the stitches and give the earrings a more finished look.

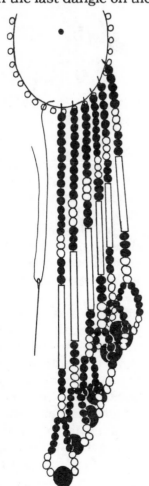

Figure 12-17

Star Rosette Earrings

56

Star Rosette Brooch

Materials Required

Nymo Thread - Size B
Long Beading Needles - Size 12
Short Beading Needles - Size 12
1 Cabochon - 18 mm x 14 mm
Seed Beads - Size 10/°
28 Round Stone Beads - 4 or 5 mm
Bar Pin - 1 1/2"
Plastic - 2" x 1 1/2"
Leather - 2" x 2 1/2"

This brooch is a classic piece of jewelry and made with black and silver rocaille beads and an onyx cabochon, it is a brilliant addition to any outfit. It matches the Star Rosette Earrings and the set is striking when worn together. This brooch also looks great as a scarf slide. The instructions for this brooch assume familiarity with the Cabochon Design Instructions. Read this section before attempting the project. Many of these techniques are also described in the first two Cabochon projects.

Getting Started

Firmly glue the cabochon to a piece of pellon mounted in an embroidery hoop. Leave at least a half inch of space around the stone. To simplify the instructions, it is assumed that the long axis of the stone is horizontal. Allow the glue to dry for at least an hour.

Lightly draw the solid pencil guidelines shown in Figure 13-1. These lines will be used to keep the beadwork straight, so make straight, accurately centered lines. They must be drawn

Figure 13-1

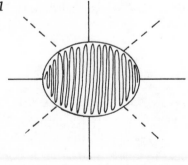

lightly or they will show through when the silver beads are stitched over them. The lines should be 1/2 inch long; the vertical lines at the top and bottom of the stone, and the horizontal lines on each side are at right angles to one another and would cross in the center of the stone if continued. Draw the dotted guidelines so that they

divide the areas between the solid guidelines in half and are at 45° angles to the solid lines. Alternatively, the guidelines can be drawn on the back of the pellon with a pen, passing through the center of the stone, and then traced lightly on the front with a pencil.

Beading the Rosette

Thread a long beading needle and tie an anchor knot in one end. Bring the needle up through the pellon just to the left of the top

Figure 13-2

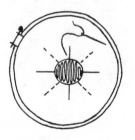

guideline, as close to the stone as possible. The thread should be positioned so that the first bead added will sit on top of this vertical guideline (Figure 13-2).

The first row consists of all silver rocaille beads. Break the row into eight strings of about 7 or 8 beads each and use an overlaid stitch to sew them to the pellon around the cabochon. Each string should end on or just past one of the guidelines. Remember to run the thread through

Figure 13-3

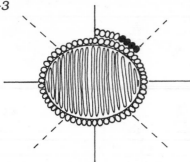

the first bead in the row before stitching down the last string of beads. When the row is complete, take a positioning stitch. Start next to the stone between the first and last beads, and emerge just outside the beads, on the top guideline so that the first bead in the second row will be to the right of this line (Figure 13-3).

Start the second row by stringing 5 silver and 4 black beads on the thread and then stitch them to the pellon. The first silver bead should sit just right of the solid vertical guideline and the last black bead should sit on the dotted guideline (see Figure 13-3). Follow the bead pattern in Figure 13-4 and add seven more strings of beads around the stone. Note that the ten silver beads in each silver section straddle the solid guidelines (5 on each side), while the middle bead of the seven in each black section sits on a dotted

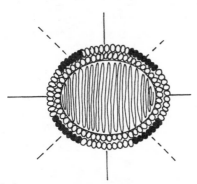

Figure 13-4

guideline. Substitute thicker or thinner beads as needed to maintain the design. Small adjustments in bead position can also be made when stitching the beads to the pellon.

When the second row is completed, take a positioning stitch to start the third row so that the first bead will sit on the solid vertical guideline.

The middle bead of the five in each silver

section of the third row sits on a solid guideline and the beads in the black sections straddle the dotted guidelines with 7 beads on each side (Figure 13-5). Divide the row into 8 strings of 9 or 10 beads each and stitch them around the cabochon. It may be necessary to add or delete a black bead or two in order to maintain the pattern of the

Figure 13-5

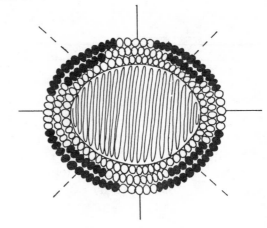

design. Keep the number of silver beads consistent with the instructions. Take a positioning stitch at the end of the row so that the first bead in the fourth row will be just to the right of the top vertical guideline.

The fourth row is the outside row of the rosette, and as such, it must be beaded with a reverse overlaid stitch. This is necessary to protect the threads from being cut when the rosette is removed from the pellon. This row consists of 8 strings of about 11 beads. Two silver beads straddle each of the solid guidelines in this

Figure 13-6

58

row (Figure 13-6). Add or delete black beads as needed to maintain the design.

Come back through the last string of beads and take the thread down through the pellon between the two outer rows of beads. Tie a finishing knot on the back of the beadwork.

Cut the beadwork out of the pellon, trimming close to the beads. Be careful not to cut any threads.

Mounting the Rosette

Place the rosette, beaded side up, on the thin piece of plastic. Outline the rosette on the plastic with a pen. Remove the rosette and use a ruler to mark several points 1/8 inch inside the first line. Draw a second line, 1/8 inch inside the

Figure 13-7

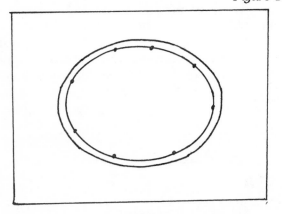

first line, using the marks as a guide (Figure 13-7).

Cut an oval out of the plastic along the inside line. The oval is smaller than the beadwork so that the pellon can be sewn to the leather backing without having to go through the plastic. Place the oval on the back of the beadwork and make sure that there is pellon visible all the way around the plastic. Trim the plastic if necessary.

Glue the plastic to the back of the beadwork, making sure it is centered. Allow the glue to dry for about an hour.

Leather Backing

Smear the rough side of the leather with an even layer of glue. Center the plastic/pellon side of the rosette on the leather and push it down firmly (Figure 13-8). Allow the glue to dry for at least an hour.

Figure 13-8

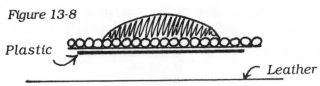

Plastic

Leather

Trim the leather around the rosette, once again cutting close to the beads. Again, do not cut any of the beadwork threads.

Use a running stitch and a short beading needle to sew the leather and pellon together all the way around the rosette. Stitch between the two outer rows of beadwork and use the needle nosed pliers to pull the needle through the leather if necessary. End with the needle and thread on the beaded side of the rosette near the right horizontal guideline. Run the needle through a black bead in the outer row, near this guideline.

Edging the Rosette

Switch to a long beading needle on the thread. Choose approximately 40 beads of each color (black and silver) which are very uniform in thickness. Use a loop edging stitch and bead all the way around the rosette, forcing the silver beads to the top of each stitch. Connect the ends of the edging by stringing 1 silver bead on the thread and running the needle down through the first black bead of the edging.

When the edging is complete, push the needle through the pellon and leather to the back of the rosette, between the last two rows of beading on the rosette.

The Dangles

These dangles are made with black and silver seed beads and 4 mm onyx beads. Turn the beadwork leather side up, with the thread in the middle of the left side of the rosette. Take a stitch sideways through the leather, emerging at the side edge.

String the following beads on the thread for the first dangle: 6 black and 4 silver seed beads; 1 4 mm onyx bead; 4 silver, 10 black and 4 silver seed beads; 1 4 mm onyx bead; 4 silver, 10 black, and 4 silver seed beads.

Bring the needle back up to the first 4 mm onyx bead (Figure 13-9), and run the thread through this bead and the rest of the beads above it in the dangle. This creates an attractive loop in the bottom of the dangle and also secures the end.

59

At the top of this string of beads, take a small (1/16 inch) sideways stitch in the leather,

Figure 13-9

from the edge of the leather towards the center of the stone (Figure 13-10). Adjust the tension in the thread so that the beads in the dangle swing freely. Take another small stitch, ending on the

Figure 13-10

edge of the leather, 1/8 inch to the right of the first dangle and make a securing stitch.

Continue adding dangles around the bottom half of the rosette, using the same bead sequence in each one. Sew each dangle to the leather using the technique described above, with 1/8 inch and a securing stitch between each dangle. The last dangle should be attached on the right side of the beadwork, in the center (Figure 13-11). Secure the end of the thread with a finishing knot at the edge of the leather.

Figure 13-11

The Pin Back

The final step is attaching the bar pin back, with glue and thread, to the back of the brooch. First, lay the pin on the back of the rosette, centering it along the horizontal guidelines with the closure on the left as shown in

Figure 13-12

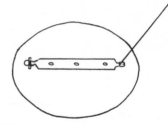

Figure 13-12. Mark the position of the pin on the leather with pencil marks on all four sides.

Remove the pin and apply a thin, even layer of glue to the back of the pin. Put the pin back on the leather, inside the pencil marks, and press it down firmly. Allow the glue to dry for at least one hour.

Thread a short beading needle with about 18 inches of thread and tie an anchor knot in one end of the thread. Coat the knot with clear

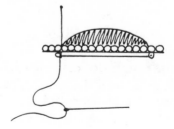

Figure 13-13

60

Figure 13-14

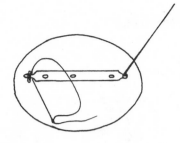

fingernail polish.

Push the needle through the rosette, going from front to back, just above the left horizontal guideline, between the stone cabochon and the first row of beadwork (Figure 13-13). Use the needle nosed pliers to pull the needle through the pellon, plastic and leather. Pull the knot down

Figure 13-15

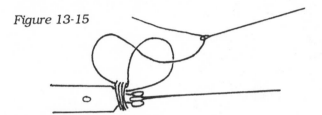

between the beads and the cabochon to hide it.

Open the closure and swing the pin por-

tion of the bar pin out of the way. Stitch over the end of the pin back (Figure 13-14), then take the needle back through all three layers of the rosette. Work the needle between the beads on the front of the rosette; use the pliers to pull it through if needed. Pull the thread tight around the narrow neck of the pin back. Take five more

Figure 13-16

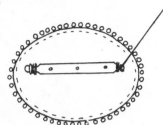

stitches over the end of the pin back, then secure the end of the thread with a finishing knot tied to the stitches (Figure 13-15). Coat the knot with clear fingernail polish.

Stitch the other end of the pin back to the rosette in the same manner (Figure 13-16). The brooch is ready to wear when the glue is completely dry.

Star Rosette Brooch

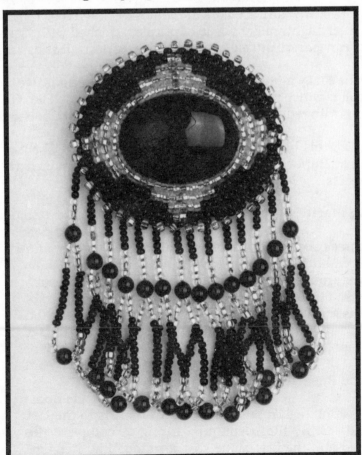

Iridescent Earrings and Necklace

Materials Required

Nymo Thread - Size B
Long Beading Needles - Size 12
Short Beading Needles - Size 12
Glover's Needle
2 Stone Cabochons - 8 mm x 6 mm
1 Stone Cabochon - 12 mm x 10 mm
Size 11/° Seed Beads
17 Bugle Beads - Size 3
20 Round Stone Beads - 4 mm
20 Pony Beads - Size 5
2 Steel Earring Pads with Posts & Nuts - 6 mm
Plastic - 2" x 2"
Leather - 4" x 2"
1 Bead Stringing Kit - Size 4
2 Bead Tips with .031" holes
1 Round Jump Ring - 4 mm
1 Spring Ring - 6 mm

This attractive set of jewelry is a simple pattern made elegant by the choice of stones and complimentary bead colors. The secrets are the iridescent, rainbow sheen of iris seed beads and using bead shades which highlight the natural colors in the stone cabochons. In this case, Cape Amethyst cabochons, which are a very light, milky shade of purple, are used with transparent amethyst iris, luster light purple, and transparent purple beads. The set works well as casual wear and for dressier affairs as well.

The pattern can be easily altered to different color combinations, with different stones in the centers. Choose bead colors which go well together and which look good next to the stones. Examples of this are jade cabochons with red and gold beads, or mother of pearl cabochons with black and white (or grey) beads.

The instructions for this brooch assume familiarity with the Cabochon Design Instructions. Read this section before attempting the project. Many of these techniques are also illustrated in the first two Cabochon projects.

Getting Started

Firmly glue all three cabochons to a piece of pellon mounted in an embroidery hoop. Leave at least 3/8 inch of space around each stone. To simplify the instructions, it is assumed that the long axis of each stone is vertical. Clean off any excess glue from around the stones and allow them to dry for at least an hour.

Beading the Rosettes

Thread a long beading needle and tie an anchor knot in one end. Bring the needle up through the pellon as close to the first stone as possible. Use an overlaid stitch and add a row of amethyst iris seed beads around the cabochon. Divide the row into four strands of about 8 beads each. Since there is no bead pattern, the position of each bead is not critical. Concentrate on stitching nice even rows that sit tightly against the stone and help hold it in place.

Adjust the number of beads in the last string to complete the row smoothly. Remem-

Figure 14-1

ber to connect the end of the row to the beginning by running the needle through the first bead in the row (Figure 14-1). Push the needle down through the pellon on the far side of this bead and stitch down the last string of beads. When the

Figure 14-2

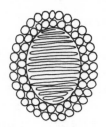

row is complete, take a small positioning stitch, emerging a half a bead width outside of the last bead added.

The second row is the outside row of the beadwork, and as such, it must be beaded with a reverse overlaid stitch. Stitch a second row of amethyst iris beads around the stone (Figure 14-2).

When this row is completed, take the thread down through the pellon between the two rows of beads and tie a finishing knot on the back of the rosette. Clip off any excess thread and coat the knot with clear fingernail polish.

Repeat the two rows of amethyst iris seed beads around the other two stones. Knot the thread on the back of each one.

Mounting the Rosettes

Glue the 6 mm earring pads to the backs of the earring rosettes, slightly above center so that the earrings will hang straight when worn

Figure 14-3

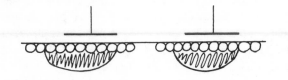

(Figure 14-3). Allow the glue to dry for at least an hour.

Cut the beadwork out of the pellon. Leave

about 1/8 inch of extra pellon around each earring rosette, but trim close to the beadwork on the necklace rosette. Be careful not to cut any threads.

Cut a plastic oval which is 1/16 inch smaller than the necklace rosette and glue it (centered) to the back of this piece.

Leather Backing

Place the leather, rough side up, on the styrofoam. Position all three rosettes on the leather so that they do not overlap. Punch two holes for the earring posts with a Glover's needle. Glue the three rosettes to the leather, pushing the earring posts through the holes in the leather and into the styrofoam. Firmly press the beadwork on the leather.

Remove the leather and beadwork from the styrofoam and cut it into three pieces, with one stone on each piece. Clean off the posts and press the leather and pellon together again, sealing the edges tightly.

When the glue has dried, cut the beadwork out of the leather. Trim the pellon and leather close to the beads. From this point on each rosette is finished separately and all beading must be completed before moving to the next piece.

Use a running stitch and a short beading needle to sew the leather and pellon together all the way around the rosette. Stitch between the two outer rows of beadwork. End with the needle and thread on the beaded side of the rosette. Run the needle through the bottom center bead in the outer row.

Edging the Rosettes

Switch to a long beading needle on the thread coming out of the bottom of the rosette. Choose at least 20 beads of each color (amethyst iris & light purple) which are uniform in thickness and size. Use a loop edging stitch and bead all the way around the rosette, forcing the light purple beads to the top of each stitch. Work in a counterclockwise direction.

Push the needle between the rows of beadwork to the back. The rosettes can be finished at this point by tying a finishing knot on the back. This creates button rosettes which are very comfortable and attractive for everyday wear.

Figure 14-4

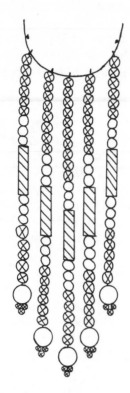

O Amethyst
⊗ Purple

▯ Bugle

O Stone

To add the beautiful, classy look of long dangles to the earrings, continue on to the next step.

Earring Dangles

The dangles are made with seed beads, bugle beads and 4 mm stone beads. Use Figure 14-4 as a guide when adding the dangles.

With the needle on the leather side of the earring, take a small stitch down to the edge of the leather. This is the point at which the middle dangle will be added, so be sure the thread is in the exact center of the bottom of the earring.

For the first dangle, string the following beads on the thread: 10 amethyst and 3 light purple seed beads; 1 purple bugle bead; 3 light purple and 5 amethyst seed beads; 1 4 mm Cape Amethyst stone bead; and 3 amethyst seed beads.

Bring the needle back up to the 4 mm stone bead and run the thread through this bead and the rest of the beads above it in the dangle. This creates a three bead loop in the bottom of the dangle and secures the end.

When the needle emerges from the top of the strand of beads, run the needle back up into the leather, emerging about 1/16 inch above the entrance point.

Adjust the tension in the thread through the dangle. Put the needle back into the leather, angling it to come out of the edge of the leather at a point that is 1/8 inch to one side of the first dangle.

Make a securing stitch and string on the beads for the second dangle. These are the same as for the first dangle, except that two amethyst beads are omitted from the top section to taper the bottom of the fringe. Use the procedure just described to complete the second dangle.

Add a third dangle on this side, omitting four amethyst beads from the top section. After the tension has been adjusted, anchor this dangle with a securing stitch and tie a finishing knot at the edge of the leather.

Thread a fresh piece of thread on a long beading needle and tie an anchor knot in one end of the thread. One eighth inch on the other side of the middle dangle, put the needle through the earring, from front to back, between the two rows of beadwork. Pull the knot down between the rows of beads. Put the needle down through the leather, emerging at the edge, ready to string on the next dangle.

Add two dangles on this side of the earring, using the same bead sequences and procedures as on the first side. Secure the thread with a finishing knot.

Finish beading the second earring. When adding the dangles, be sure they match the lengths and taper of the dangles on the first earring.

The Necklace

The dangles for the necklace are done in the same manner as for the earrings, but instead of five dangles, seven are added, one extra on each side. The extra dangles have the following bead sequence: 5 amethyst and 3 light purple seed beads; 1 purple bugle bead; 3 light purple and 4 amethyst seed beads; 1 Cape Amethyst stone bead; and 3 amethyst seed beads.

When the dangles are finished, the beaded necklace string and clasp can be added. In addition to the beads already used in the necklace, the necklace string contains transparent purple pony beads.

Figure 14-5

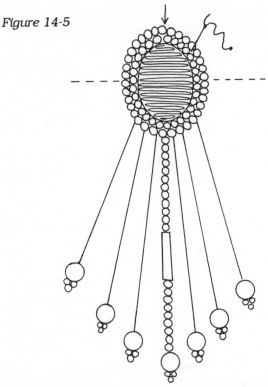

Figure 14-6

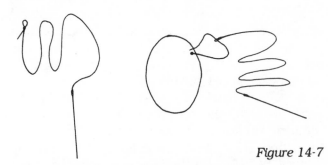

this color scheme. Tie a loop knot in the end of the cord which does not have the needle attached to it, however, do not tighten the knot all the way. Instead, leave a small loop in the end of the thread (Figure 14-6).

Turn the knot into an anchor knot by stacking two more loop knots on top of the first

Figure 14-7

String about 18 inches of thread on a short beading needle and tie an anchor knot in one end. The necklace string attaches to the cabochon about halfway between the top center and an imaginary line drawn horizontally through the center of the stone. Find this point on the left side of the beadwork and push the needle between the two rows of beads to the back of the piece (Figure 14-5). Pull the knot down between the beads to hide it.

Take out the bead stringing kit and completely unwind the cord. Purple is a good color for

one, still leaving the single small loop in the end of the thread. Trim the loose end of the cord and paint the knot with clear fingernail polish.

Run the needle and thread attached to the necklace cabochon through the small loop at the end of the purple cord. Then put the needle back through the beadwork about 1/16 inch above the point where the thread emerges from the back of the beadwork (Figure 14-7).

Pull the thread snug, thus attaching the purple cord to the back of the beadwork. Take four or five more stitches through the small loop, firmly securing it to the beadwork. Tie a finishing knot around these stitches.

Use Figure 14-8 as a guide and string the following beads on the purple cord: 10 amethyst

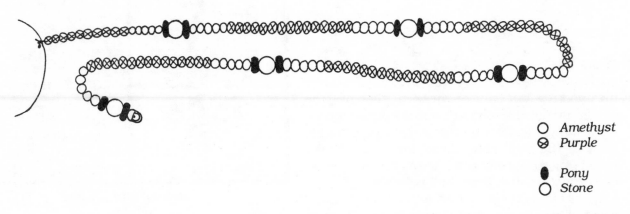

⃝	Amethyst
⊗	Purple
⬤	Pony
⃝	Stone

Figure 14-8

and 5 light purple seed beads; 1 purple pony bead, 1 Cape Amethyst stone bead and 1 purple pony bead; 5 light purple, 15 amethyst and 5 light purple seed beads; 1 purple pony bead, 1 Cape Amethyst stone bead and 1 purple pony bead; 5 light purple, 15 amethyst and 5 light purple seed beads; 1 purple pony bead, 1 Cape Amethyst stone bead; and 1 purple pony bead; 5 light purple, 15 amethyst and 5 light purple seed beads; 1 purple pony bead,1 Cape Amethyst stone bead; and 1 purple pony bead; 5 light purple, 15 amethyst and 5 light purple seed beads; 1 purple pony bead, 1 Cape Amethyst stone bead; and 1 purple pony bead.

Next, string one of the bead tips on the cord. Put a simple overhand knot in the cord near the bead tip (Figure 14-9), but before the knot is tightened, stick a heavy sewing needle in the loop (Figure 14-10). Use the needle to scoot the knot down into the cup of the bead tip (Figure 14-11), while putting enough tension on the cord to take up any slack. When the knot is in the cup of the bead tip and all the extra cord has been pulled past the knot (make sure all the beads are lined

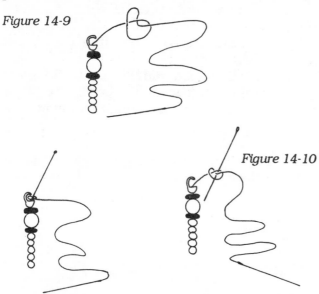

Figure 14-9

Figure 14-10

Figure 14-11

up smoothly, but snug on the cord), then pull the needle out of the loop and let the knot tighten completely. Repeat this process, creating a double knot in the cup of the bead tip. Cut off the remaining cord, close to the knot and set it aside. Coat the knot with fingernail polish.

Next, put the 4 mm jump ring over the hook of the bead tip (Figure 14-12). Use the

needle nosed pliers to close the hook of the bead tip (Figure 14-13). This completes the first half of

Figure 14-12   *Figure 14-13*

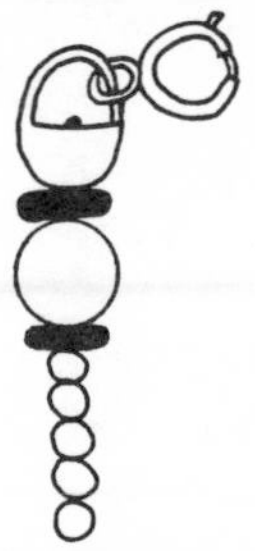

Figure 14-14

the necklace string.

The second half of the necklace string is made in the same manner as the first. Sew the remainder of the bead stringing cord to the right side of the necklace body, making sure that this second cord is attached directly across the beadwork from the first one, so that the necklace will hang evenly when worn.

String the same number and sequence of beads on the cord, and attach the second bead tip. Put the 6 mm spring ring over the hook of the bead tip, and close the hook with the needle nosed pliers (Figure 14-14). Hook the spring ring into the jump ring and the necklace is finished.

Iridescent Earrings and Necklace

Starburst Rosette Earrings and Bolo Tie

Materials Required

Nymo Thread - Size B
Long Beading Needles - Size 12 & Size 13
Short Beading Needles - Size 12
Glover's Needle
3 Stone Cabochons - 10 mm x 12 mm
Seed Beads - Size 12/° & Size 10/°
18 Bugle Beads - Size 3
18 Stone Beads - 4 or 5 mm
Earring Pads with Posts & Nuts - 14 mm
Bolo Cord & Back - 3/4" round pad or locking back
Plastic - 2" x 2"
Leather - 3" x 6"

The pattern for this jewelry set is similar to the Star Rosettes, but the detail is finer and the design more elaborate. The color scheme of turquoise stones with cream, rust, black, sea green and turquoise blue beads gives the set a very different look from the star rosettes and has a decidedly Western flavor. These are guaranteed to get lots of compliments.

A brooch can be made instead of a bolo tie; simply substitute a 1 1/2 inch bar pin for the bolo cord and back. One hank of each size and color bead will be enough to make all three pieces. For a more rustic look, stone chips, with holes drilled in them, can be substituted for the round stone beads. The instructions for these rosettes assume familiarity with the Cabochon Design Instructions. Read this section before attempting this project. Many of these techniques are also illustrated in the first two Cabochon projects.

Getting Started

Firmly glue all three cabochons to a piece of pellon mounted in an embroidery hoop. Leave at least a half inch of open space around each earring stone and at least 3/4 inch around the bolo stone (Figure 15-1). To simplify the instructions, it is assumed that the long axis of each stone is vertical. Allow the glue to dry for at least an hour.

Draw the solid pencil guidelines shown in Figure 15-2 around each stone. These lines will be used to keep the beadwork straight, so make straight, accurately centered lines. The lines around the earring stones should be 1/2 inch long and the lines around the bolo stone should be 3/4 inch long; the vertical lines at the top and bottom of the stones, and the horizontal lines on each side are at right angles to one another and would cross in the center of the stone if continued. Draw the dotted guidelines so that they divide the areas between the solid guidelines in half and are at 45° angles to the solid lines.

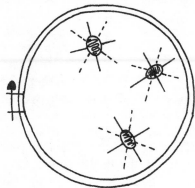

Figure 15-1

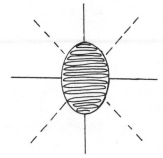

Figure 15-2

Beading the Rosettes

All three rosettes have the same color pattern for the first four rows. This pattern is shown in Figure 15-3 and should be referred to while beading the design to make sure it is correct. Use size 12/° seed beads to make the

Figure 15-3

body of each rosette and bead the two earring stones first.

Thread a size 13 long beading needle and tie an anchor knot in one end. Bring the needle up through the pellon to the left of the top guideline, as close to the stone as possible. The thread should be positioned so that the first two

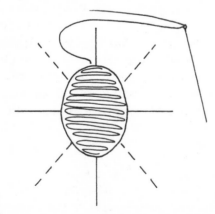

Figure 15-4

beads added will straddle the top guideline (Figure 15-4).

The first row consists of all cream colored beads. Break the row into four strings of about 8 beads each and use an overlaid stitch to sew them

to the pellon around the cabochon. Remember to run the thread through the first bead in the row before stitching down the last string of beads. When the row is complete, take a positioning stitch. Start next to the stone between the first and second beads and emerge just outside the beads,

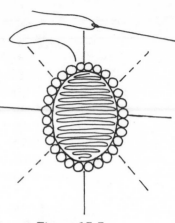

Figure 15-5

to the left of the top solid guideline so that the first two beads in the second row will straddle this guideline (Figure 15-5).

Start the second row by stringing: 2 cream, 1 rust brown, 2 turquoise blue, 1 black, 2 turquoise blue, 1 rust brown, and 2 cream beads on the thread. The two sets of cream beads must straddle the solid guidelines and the black bead should sit on top of the dotted guideline.

Spend the time needed to get just the right beads in each portion of the pattern; the difference in the appearance of the finished beadwork will be well worth the effort. Remember that it is more important to maintain crisp definition of the pattern than it is to use the exact number of beads in the instruc-

Figure 15-6

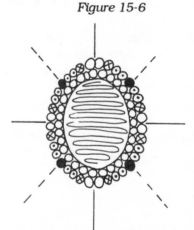

tions. If beads must be added or deleted this will be least noticeable in the sea green background, so try to make all adjustments in this area of the design.

Follow the color pattern in Figure 15-6 and add the other three strings of beads in this row with the same overlaid stitch. Each string should be 7 to 9 beads in length and it is easiest if they end on or just past a solid guideline. The Star Rosette project provides an example of how to divide the rows. End the row with a positioning stitch so that the first bead in the third row will sit on the top guideline rather than next to it.

The cream beads in the third row should all sit on top of the guidelines (Figure 15-7). Pay attention to the pattern emerging for each color in the design and compare it to Figure 15-3. Divide

Figure 15-9

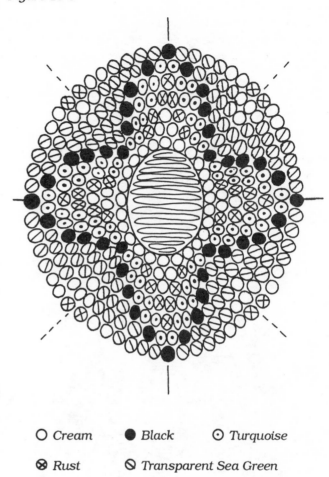

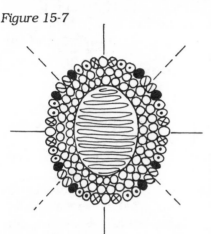

Figure 15-7

the row into four strings of about 11 beads; it will be easiest to end with the single cream beads which sit on the solid guidelines. If the strings have too many beads to handle comfortably, split them in half before stitching them down. Take a positioning stitch at the end of the third row so that the first two beads in the next row will straddle the top guideline.

The rust beads in the fourth row must straddle each of the guidelines (Figure 15-8). Divide the row into four strings of 12 to 15 beads each and sew them to the pellon with a reverse overlaid stitch on the two earring stones. Con-

| ○ Cream | ● Black | ⊙ Turquoise |
| ⊗ Rust | ◒ Transparent Sea Green |

the bolo rosette. The finished design is shown in Figure 15-9.

In the fifth row (Figure 15-10) a single rust brown bead sits on top of each of the solid guidelines and single cream beads are positioned on top of the dotted guidelines. The row starts on the top guideline and consists of four strings of about 14 beads. Add this row in the same manner as the previous ones, checking the positions of the beads before stitching down each string. Take a positioning stitch at the end of the row, so that the first bead of the next row will be just to the left of the top guideline.

The sixth row of beadwork is shown in Figure 15-11. The row starts with two turquoise blue beads which straddle the top guideline. Turquoise beads also straddle the other solid guidelines. The middle bead of each cream section sits on a dotted guideline, directly above the single cream beads in the previous row. Divide the row into four strings of 14 to 16 beads

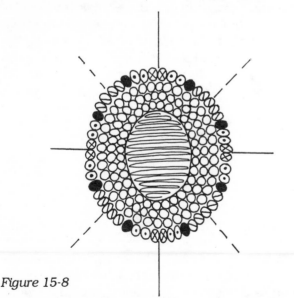

Figure 15-8

tinue to use a regular overlaid stitch for this row on the bolo stone. Secure the end of the thread with a finishing knot on the back of each of the two earring stones.

Three more rows of beadwork are added to

Figure 15-10

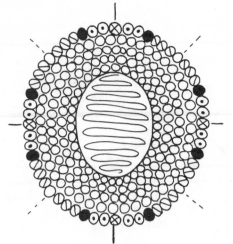

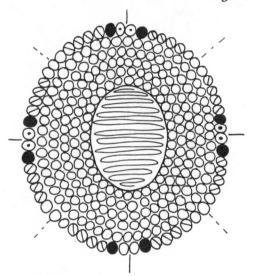

Figure 15-11

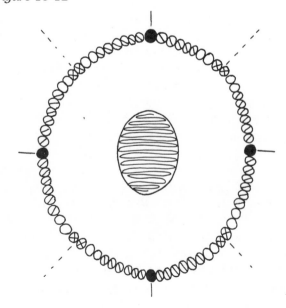

Figure 15-12

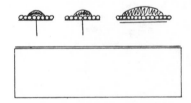

and stitch them to the pellon.

The seventh row is the last, so use a reverse overlaid stitch. In this row a single black bead sits on top of each solid guideline and two rust brown beads straddle each dotted guideline (Figure 15-12). Use four strands of 17 to 19 beads or eight strands of 7 to 9 beads if working with fewer beads is more comfortable. Secure the thread with a finishing knot on the back of the rosette.

Mounting the Rosettes

Glue the 14 mm earring pads to the backs of the earring rosettes, slightly above center so that the earrings will hang straight when worn. Allow the glue to dry for at least an hour.

Cut the beadwork out of the pellon. Leave about 1/8 inch of extra pellon around each earring rosette, but trim close to the beadwork on the bolo rosette. Be careful not to cut any threads.

Cut a plastic oval which is 1/16 inch smaller than the bolo rosette and glue it (centered) to the back of this piece.

Leather Backing

Place the leather, rough side up, on the styrofoam. Position all three rosettes on the leather so that they do not overlap. Punch two holes for the earring posts with a Glover's needle. Glue the three rosettes to the leather, pushing the earring posts through the holes in the leather and into the styrofoam (Figure 15-13). Firmly press

Figure 15-13

the beadwork on the leather.

Remove the leather and beadwork from the styrofoam. Cut the leather into three pieces with one stone on each piece. Clean off the posts and press the leather and pellon together again, sealing the edges tightly on all three pieces of beadwork.

When the glue has dried, cut the beadwork out of the leather. Trim the pellon and leather close to the beads. From this point on, each

rosette is finished separately and all beading must be completed on each piece before moving to the next one.

Use a running stitch and a short beading needle to sew the leather and pellon together all the way around the rosette. Stitch between the two outer rows of beadwork. End with the needle and thread on the beaded side of the rosette at the bottom. Run the needle through the bottom bead (rust on the earrings, black on the bolo) in the outer row.

Edging the Rosettes

Switch to a long beading needle on the thread coming out the bottom of the rosette. Use size 10/° seed beads for the rest of the beading except where specifically noted.

Choose about 30 beads of each color (cream and rust brown) which are uniform in thickness and size. Use a loop edging stitch and bead all the way around the rosette, forcing the cream beads to the top of each stitch.

On the bolo rosette, push the needle through the rows of beadwork and tie a finishing knot on the back of the rosette. The earrings can also be finished in this manner, creating button rosettes which are very comfortable and attractive for everyday wear. To add the beautiful, classy look of long dangles to the earrings, continue on to the next step.

The Dangles

The dangles are made with seed beads, bugle beads and 4 mm stone beads. Start at the bottom of the rosette, in the center and push the needle through to the leather side. Take a stitch

Figure 15-14

down through just the leather, emerging at the bottom edge.

String the following beads on the thread for the first dangle: 15 rust brown, 2 cream, 2 sea green, 1 black, and 2 turquoise blue size 10/° seed beads; 1 black bugle bead; 2 turquoise blue, 1 black, 2 sea green, 2 cream, and 5 rust brown size 10/° seed beads; 1 4 mm turquoise stone bead; and 3 cream size 12/° seed beads (Figure 15-14).

Start at the 4 mm turquoise bead and run the needle back up through all the beads in the dangle except the last three. The beads on the end of the dangle will form a loop, securing the thread at the bottom of the dangle.

Take a small vertical stitch in the leather (about 1/16 inch), entering close to the hole from which the thread for this dangle emerged. Adjust the tension in the dangle so that the beads swing freely. Take a small angled stitch, ending on the edge of the leather, 1/8 inch to the right of the first dangle and make a securing stitch before adding the beads for the next dangle.

Add four more dangles on this side of the earring, using the procedure just described. Taper the bottoms by omitting 3 or 4 rust brown beads from the top section of each successive dangle. The

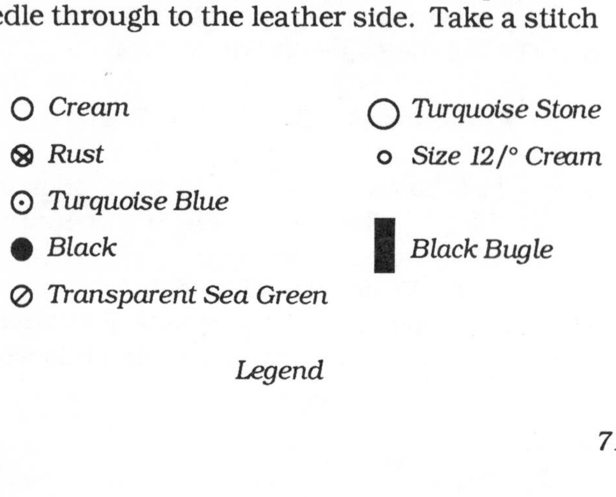

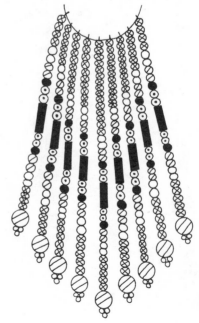

Figure 15-15

○ Cream

⊗ Rust

☉ Turquoise Blue

● Black

⊘ Transparent Sea Green

○ Turquoise Stone

∘ Size 12/° Cream

▌ Black Bugle

Legend

71

thickness of the beads will determine how many beads must be omitted in order to achieve a uniform taper. Figure 15-15 shows the bead sequence and how the taper should look. When the last dangle on this side of the earring is secured, tie a finishing knot on the back edge of the rosette.

Thread the needle with a fresh piece of knotted thread. Push the needle through the rosette from the beaded side, 1/8 inch to the left of the middle dangle. Take a small vertical stitch to the bottom edge of the leather and string the next dangle on the thread. The dangles on this side of the earring mirror those on the first side (see Figure 15-15). Add all four dangles to this side of the rosette, making sure the taper remains even. Secure the end of the thread with a finishing knot on the back of the rosette.

When the dangles are added to the second earring make sure that the lengths of the dangles are the same on both earrings.

Alternate Dangles

This fringe substitutes the unique look of porcupine quills for the bugle beads used above. The larger loop at the bottom gives the earrings a fuller look, which many people prefer. All the materials, except the porcupine quills, should already be on hand.

Directions for preparing porcupine quills are given in the General Instructions. This should be done before work on the dangles begins. Cut the quills 1/2 inch long for medium length dangles and 3/4 inch long for long dangles. These dangles are added in the same manner as the original dangles described for this project.

With the thread in position for the center dangle string the following beads on the thread: 15 rust brown, 2 cream, 2 sea green, 1 black and 2 turquoise blue seed beads; 1 porcupine quill; 2 turquoise blue, 1 black, 2 sea green, 2 cream, and 5 rust brown seed beads; 1 4 mm turquoise stone bead; 5 rust brown, 2 cream, 2 sea green and 1 black seed bead (Figure 15-16).

To create the loop at the bottom of the dangle, re-enter the line of beads at the second turquoise blue seed bead below the quill. Run the needle back up through the rest of the dangle and into the leather as previously described (Figure 15-17). Be careful to equalize the tension up and down the fringe to get a uniform loop.

Add four more dangles to the first side of the earring, putting three or four fewer rust brown beads in the top section of each successive dangle.

Return to the center of the rosette and add four more dangles to the other side of the earring. Make sure the taper is equal on both sides of the earring. Again, make sure that the lengths of the dangles are the same on both earrings.

Finishing the Bolo Tie or Brooch

Two kinds of bolo backs are shown in Figure 15-18. The round, single piece kind is shown in (a) and the pieces of the locking type are shown in (b). Either can be used, but the locking mechanism on the three piece back does not slip and it keeps the bolo straighter when it is worn.

Figure 15-16   *Figure 15-17*

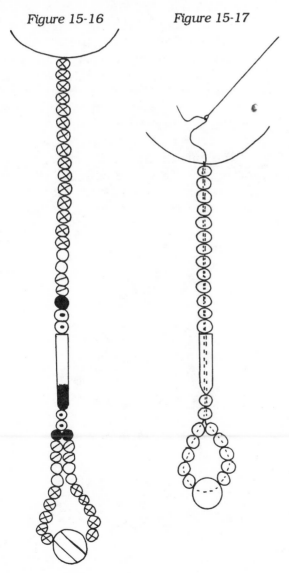

Figure 15-18a

Figure 15-18b

the bolo cord into the top holders of the pad, over the wings of the locking piece, and down through the bottom holders of the pad. Pull the two cord ends through, leaving a loop at the top of the rosette (Figure 15-22). Release the pressure on the locking mechanism and the cord will be held firmly in place. To move the rosette up and down

Figure 15-21

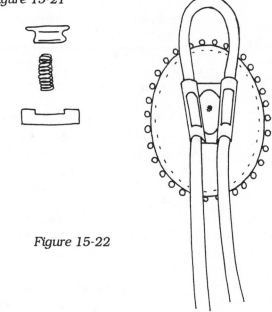

For either type, glue the flat side of the bolo pad (the piece which the cord slides through) to the leather backing of the beadwork, slightly above center on one end of the oval rosette (Figure 15-19). The wide end of the piece from the locking type is the top. Use more glue than with an earring pad and wait for one minute before sticking the pad to the leather. Allow the glue to dry overnight.

For a single piece back, use needle nosed pliers to open the curved bolo holders on the pad. Slide the cord under

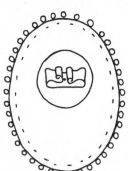

Figure 15-19

Figure 15-22

them, leaving a loop of bolo cord at the top (Figure 15-20). Adjust the tension of the holders on the cord with the pliers so that the rosette slides when pushed, but does not slip on its own.

For a locking back, stand the spring over the hole in the bolo pad, then place the locking piece over the spring, so that its hole is over the top of the spring (Figure 15-21). Push the locking piece down into the pad. Hold it down and thread the ends of

Figure 15-20

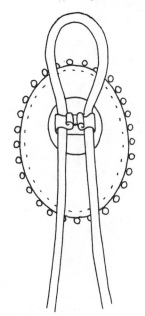

the cord, push down on the locking piece and pull the rosette in the desired direction.

To make a brooch, glue a 1 1/2 inch bar pin to the center of the leather backing on the rosette. Stitch the ends of the pin to the leather backing, through the holes provided or over the ends of the pin (Figures 15-23 and 15-24). Allow

Figure 15-23

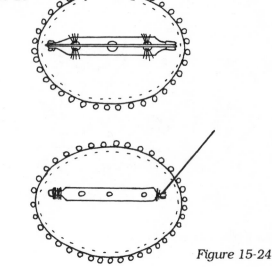

Figure 15-24

the glue to dry overnight and the brooch is ready to wear.

Beading the Bolo Cord Tips

To put the finishing touch on the bolo tie and make it really special, bead the ends of the cord in a matching color pattern. The peyote or barrel stitch (see Peyote Design Instructions) is ideally suited for this work.

Begin with a foundation row of 12 rust brown seed beads (size 12/°) tied loosely together with a loop knot.

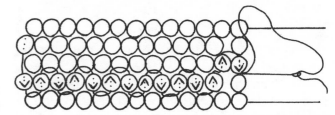

Tip

Figure 15-25

Slip the ring of beads over the end of the bolo cord. About 2 inches up the cord, draw the ring tight around the cord by pulling the ends of the thread in opposite directions.

Put a second needle on the short piece of thread and run it through several of the beads to hide and secure this end. Remove the needle and clip off any excess thread.

Hold the cord in one hand with the plastic wrapped tip of the cord facing up (Figure 15-25) and bead up towards the end of the cord.

Follow the color sequence in Figure 15-26 and bead the second row with rust brown beads and a peyote stitch. Make a step up stitch at the end of the row. The next three rows are beaded with turquoise blue beads with a step up at the end of each row.

Continue in the same manner, adding the following rows of beads (see Figure 15-26): two rows of black beads; two rows of sea green beads;

Figure 15-26

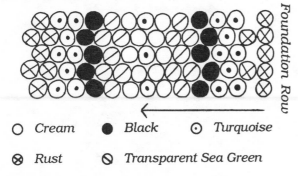

| O Cream | ● Black | ⊙ Turquoise |
| ⊗ Rust | ◒ Transparent Sea Green | |

two rows of cream beads; one row of turquoise blue beads; two rows of cream beads; two rows of

sea green beads; two rows of black beads; three rows of turquoise blue beads; and three rows of rust brown beads.

After the last row is completed, slide the beadwork up to the end of the bolo cord. Run the needle through all the beads in the last row again. Pull it tight over the end of the bolo cord. Run the needle through these beads one more time and pull the thread tight, making the beads snug over the end of the bolo cord.

Figure 15-27

Invert the beadwork and weave the thread up through the beads to the foundation row, now at the top of the beadwork (Figure 15-27).

Push the needle through the bolo cord itself, then take the needle back through one of the beads in the foundation row. Repeat this procedure through several foundation row beads, until the beadwork is securely anchored to the bolo cord.

Weave the thread back down into the body of the beadwork. Pass through several beads in different rows so the thread will not work loose. Clip off any excess thread and coat the area of the beadwork with the end of the thread woven into it with clear fingernail polish.

Starburst Rosette Earring & Bolo

Applique Designs

Rosebud Barrette or Brooch

Materials Required

Nymo Thread - Size B
Long Beading Needles - Size 13
Short Beading Needles - Size 12
Cut Seed Beads - Size 12/°
Seed Beads - Size 13/°
Barrette Back or Bar Pin - 2 1/4"
Plastic - 3" x 3"
Leather - 3" x 3"

Nothing looks better in hair than a dazzling piece of beadwork. This lovely piece never goes out of style and is a practical way of keeping one's hair under control.

This project uses the overlaid stitch described in the Cabochon Design Instructions to outline and fill a pattern drawn on fabric. The technique is similar to embroidery and is called applique. Many embroidery patterns adapt well to this kind of beadwork and these techniques can also be used to bead original designs.

Opaque dark red, opaque light green, transparent gold and transparent medium green seed beads are used in combination with dark green and light red cut seed beads in this project.

Getting Started

Lay the pellon over the pattern in the book (Figure 16-1) and trace it carefully onto the pellon. The sections in the pattern are numbered in the order of beading and will be used in the text to refer the reader to the correct portion of the work. They do not have to be transferred to the pellon.

Put the pellon in an embroidery hoop. Center the pattern in the circle and stretch the cloth tight. Cut off any excess pellon from around the bottom of the hoop.

Beading the Rosebud

Thread a long beading needle and tie an anchor knot in one end of the thread. Coat this

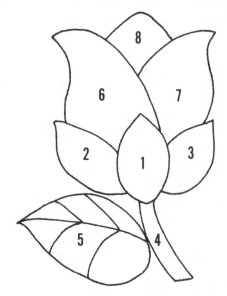

Figure 16-1

and all other knots with clear fingernail polish.

For the purpose of providing instructions, consider the flower petals as the top of the piece and the large leaf (section 5) as the left side. Bring the needle up under the hoop and through the pellon at the bottom of the central bud leaf (point A in Figure 16-2). Outline this middle bud leaf

Figure 16-2

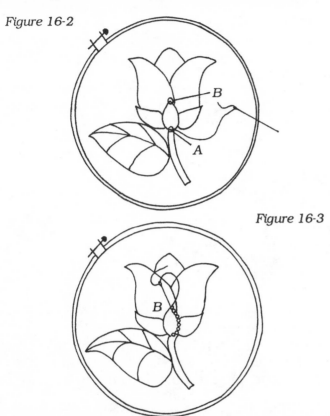

Figure 16-3

(section 1) with dark green cut seed beads and an overlaid stitch. The use of this stitch for applique is described in detail (below) for the first leaf.

String enough dark green beads on the thread to reach the tip of the leaf (point B) along the pattern outline and put the needle down through the pellon at this point (Figure 16-3).

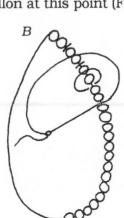

Figure 16-4

A

Stitch this string of beads to the pellon by bringing the needle back up through the pellon on the traced leaf line, two beads down from point B. Go over the thread between the second and third beads from this end and back down through the pellon on the drawn line (Figure 16-4).

Come up through the pellon two beads down from the first stitch, and once again go over the thread and back down through the pellon on the pattern line. Continue tacking down this line of beads, taking a stitch every second bead, until the starting point (A) is reached (Figure 16-5).

Bring the needle up through the pellon one bead to the right of point A and go through this bead, from right to left, positioning the thread to outline the other side of the leaf (see Figure 16-5).

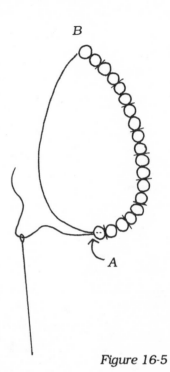

Figure 16-5

String enough dark green cut beads to reach the tip of the leaf (point B) along the pattern line on the other side of the leaf. Put the needle down through the pellon at point B again and tack down this line of beads in the same way as the first line. Finish at the starting point (A) once again. Take a positioning stitch, bringing the needle up through the pellon about one half a bead width above point A (Figure 16-6).

Figure 16-6

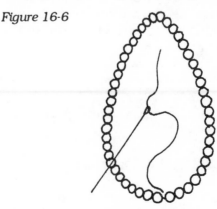

A

Figure 16-7

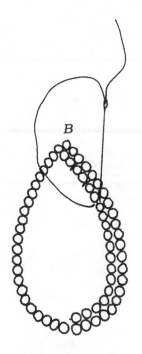

Figure 16-7

beading inward. Follow the pattern in Figure 16-8 and add another row of medium green beads. The next three rows are half medium green and half opaque light green. The light green beads in the center of the leaf give the effect of sunshine on the leaf.

As the rows are added, try to fit the beads in smoothly, without any bulging. A good rule to remember is "if the bead doesn't fit in nicely, leave it out!" A little loose is better than too tightly packed and the tacking stitches can be used to space the beads evenly.

When beading oddly shaped areas such as leaves, it may also be necessary to sew some beads in sideways to fill a small space. In this case, string the beads on the thread one at a time and stitch each one directly to the pellon. The thread for these stitches should come out of the pellon, through the bead, and back down through the pellon at whatever angle is necessary to situate the bead correctly. Pulling the thread snug will pull the bead down into the space available.

Go to the tip of the next bud leaf (section 2) by taking a small stitch or two across the back of the pellon to point A in Figure 16-9. These stitches must stay within the bounds of the drawing or they will be cut later. Outline from point A to point B and then from point C to point B with dark green cut seed beads. Bead the interior of the leaf with about three lines of beads, stitching beads in sideways where necessary. The center row should contain three or four light green beads, placed so they are in the very center of the leaf. There should be room for 1 or 2 light green beads in a partial row next to the center one.

Go to the bottom of the third bud leaf (section 3) and bring the thread up through the pellon at point A (Figure 16-10). Outline the leaf from point A to point B and then from point C to

String on enough transparent medium green beads to lay a line of them up to point B, just inside the first string of dark green beads. Put the needle down through the pellon just below point B and tack down this line of beads (Figure 16-7).

When the bottom of the leaf is reached, go through the first bead in this line (above point A) from right to left, positioning the thread to add the beads for the other half of this row.

String on enough transparent green beads to lay a line up to point B on the other side of the leaf. Put the needle down through the pellon at the same place below point B, then tack down the beads in this line to complete the second row.

Continue filling the interior of this leaf,

Figure 16-8

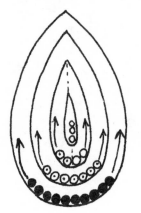

Figure 16-9

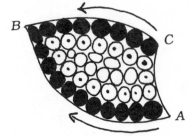

○ Lt Green
⊙ Med Green
● Dark Green

77

Figure 16-10

Figure 16-12

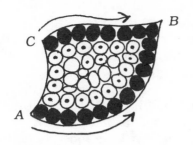

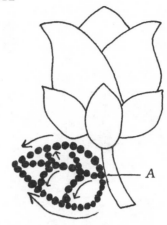

○ Lt Green
◉ Med Green
● Dark Green

point B with dark green cut seed beads. Fill the interior of the leaf with rows of medium green seed beads, using four or five light green beads in the very center of the leaf.

Go to the top of the stem (section 4). Bring the thread up through the pellon on the right edge of the stem (point A in Figure 16-11). Bead the

beads in sideways, one at a time, where necessary to fill this space. When the large leaf is completed, take the needle down through the pellon and tie a finishing knot on the back side of the piece.

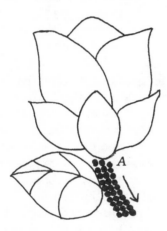

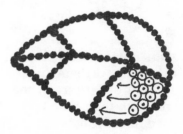

Figure 16-13

The next step is to outline the flower petals (sections 6, 7, and 8) with opaque dark red seed beads. It is easiest to outline all three petals before filling the interior of any of them. Start with petal 7 at point A in Figure 16-14 and bead

Figure 16-11

stem with three lines of dark green cut seed beads, running from the top to the bottom of the stem.

Now go to the big leaf (section 5). Bring the needle up through the pellon next to the stem, by the center vein (point A in Figure 16-12). Outline both sides of the leaf with lines of dark green cut seed beads from Point A to the tip of the leaf, then bead the central vein of the leaf with dark green beads as well. Finally, bead the four side veins with dark green; position the thread for each vein with stitches beneath the central vein and bead from the center to the edge of the leaf.

Fill in the spaces between the veins with rows of medium green transparent seed beads, following the curve of the outer leaf outline (Figure 16-13). Bead from the outside in, sewing

Figure 16-14

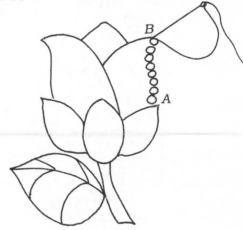

to point B.

Work the thread over to the left, top edge of petal 7 (point C in Figure 16-15). String on enough dark red beads to reach the tip of the petal (point B) and stitch them down (Figure 16-16). Divide this line into two strings of beads if there are too many to handle comfortably.

Figure 16-15

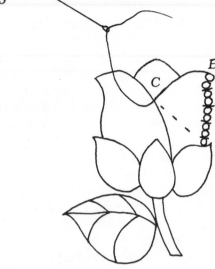

Figure 16-17

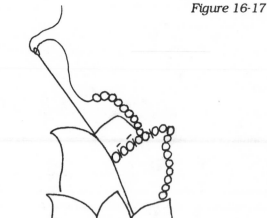

Finally, work the thread over to the bottom left corner of petal 6 and outline the left edge, again laying the beads on the pellon from bottom to top (Figure 16-19).

Figure 16-16

Figure 16-18

Bead the upper edge of the small petal (section 8) next with a single line (Figure 16-17). Take a stitch on either side of the bead at the tip of the petal to be sure that the beads remain on the pattern line. Work the thread over to the bottom right corner of petal 6 and outline the long top edge of this petal (Figure 16-18). This line can also be split into two or three strings of beads.

Bead the interior of each flower petal with medium red cut seed beads, starting at the tip of each one and beading down both sides. Follow the curves of the outline and bead inward, ending in the center of each petal (Figure 16-20). Pick out smaller or larger beads while working, in order to

79

Figure 16-19

neatly fill the space.

After the petals are completed, outline the entire piece with a single row of transparent gold beads (Figure 16-21). The outline ties the piece

Figure 16-20

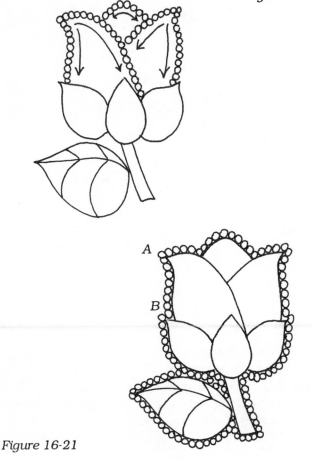

Figure 16-21

together and strengthens it; it also smooths the silhouette, which simplifies mounting the beadwork.

Start at point A (the top left corner), string on enough beads to reach the next point or corner (e.g. point B) and put the needle back through the pellon. Stitch the beads to the pellon with a reverse overlaid stitch; that is, bring the needle up on the beadwork side of the row, go over the thread connecting the beads, and put the needle back into the pellon, angling it under the beads from the far side. This tucks the outside threads well under the beads and avoids their being cut when the work is removed from the pellon.

Run the needle and thread back through the string of beads to the end point (point B). Take a small stitch in the pellon to position the thread for the next string of beads and continue around the rosebud. If there is any space remaining between the big leaf (section 5) and the rest of the piece, fill it with transparent gold beads as well. Secure the thread on the back of the piece with a finishing knot.

Cut the beadwork out of the pellon, trimming close to the beads. Be careful not to cut any threads. At this point the beadwork can be sewn on to a jacket, blouse or purse as a permanent decoration or mounted as a barrette or brooch.

Mounting the Beadwork

Lay the rosebud, beaded side up, on the piece of plastic and trace the beadwork. Remove the beadwork and draw another line 3/16 of an inch inside the first line. Cut the plastic along the inside line so that the resulting piece will be slightly smaller than the beadwork. Trim the plastic if necessary, leaving enough room to stitch the beadwork to the leather backing without having to go through the plastic. Glue the plastic (centered) to the back of the beadwork. Allow the glue to dry for at least an hour.

Next, lay the leather on a flat surface, rough side up. Place the rosebud on the leather, beaded side up, and trace the beadwork with a pencil. The pattern on the leather must be the same size as the beadwork. Cut the leather backing along the pattern line. Trim the leather piece to fit the beadwork if necessary.

Glue the rough side of the leather to the plastic side of the beadwork. Press the pieces together, sealing the edges of the leather and

pellon together. Allow the glue to dry for several hours.

Stitch the leather to the beadwork using a short beading needle and a running stitch (described in Cabochon Design Instructions). Stitch back and forth, through the beadwork and leather, all the way around the edge of the rosebud (Figure 16-22). Stay inside the row of gold beads to hide the thread on the beaded side of the work. Secure

Figure 16-22

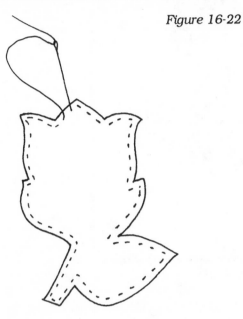

provided in the metal. Use a short beading needle and put an anchor knot in the end of the thread. Start on the beaded side and hide the knot between the beads. Use pliers to pull the needle through the leather, plastic and beadwork. Sew over the end of the metal piece with stitches in a fan shape to securely anchor the metal back (Figure 16-23). Do Not use a Glover's needle for this work as it can cut the threads of the beadwork. Secure the end of the thread with a finishing knot.

Apply some glue to the back of the metal barrette and press it down on the leather. Then stitch this end to the beadwork in the same manner as the first end. The glue can not be applied to the barrette back prior to stitching down the first end because it curves away from the leather and the glue will dry before this stitching can be completed.

To make a brooch, center the pin back on the back of the beadwork and mark all four sides with a pencil. Apply a layer of glue to the flat side of the pin back, wait one minute, then stick it inside the marks on the leather. Allow the glue to dry for at least an hour. This works because the pin back is flat. Stitch the pin back to the rosebud through the holes provided as shown in Figure 16-24. If the pin has no holes, stitch over both ends to secure it to the beadwork.

the end of the thread with a finishing knot on the back of the beadwork.

The Barrette Clip or Bar Pin

To make a barrette, center the metal barrette back on the leather side of the beadwork and stitch one end to the beadwork using the hole

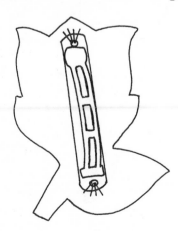

Figure 16-23

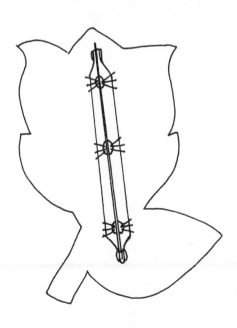

Figure 16-24

Rosebud Barrette

THE TECHNIQUES OF NORTH AMERICAN INDIAN BEADWORK
by
Monte Smith

This exciting book contains directions for selecting, buying and using beading materials; guidelines for either buying or making your own beadwork loom; and, an examination of Indian beadwork designs, their development, significance and uses.

With complete step-by-step instructions for all of the variations of beading techniques used in both loom and applique work, included are directions for beading round objects, rosettes and necklaces.

There are approximately 200 illustrations, examples and photos of beaded articles from 1835 to the present. Examples are from the Apache, Arapaho, Assiniboine, Bannock, Blackfoot, Cheyenne, Chippewa-Cree, Comanche, Cree, Crow, Flathead, Gros Ventre, Huron, Kiowa, Mohawk, Navajo, Ojibwa, Omaha, Otto, Piaute, Pottawatomi, Sac & Fox, Shoshone, Sioux, Umitilla, Ute, Winnebago and Yakima.

This is a book of 102 pages that anyone interested in Indian Beadwork will want to own and study.

NEW ADVENTURES IN BEADING EARRINGS
by
Laura Reid

This fantastic new book is fully illustrated and presents step-by-step instructions on making truly beautiful and distinctive earrings.

Written by noted craftsperson and author Laura Reid, each step is fully explained and the entire text has been "reader tested" and enthusiastically endorsed.

The styles include five-star, snowflake and cross point-style earrings; small fan, large bugle fan, large and small bugle fan, porcupine quill fan and circle fan-style earrings; and, three-square, bugle star in circle, large bugle rectangle, small bugle base, five bugle base, seven bugle base, ten bugle base and one dimensional cube square-type earrings.

All of the materials used are easily obtainable and all of the styles are based on seed beads and bugle beads. Further, from the styles explained and illustrated, and based on the easy-to-follow instructions, the reader is encouraged to go beyond the basics of the book and create their own designs.

Anyone who enjoys creating and then wearing beautiful craftwork will find this book to be a must.

EAGLE'S VIEW BESTSELLERS

☐	Eagle's View Publishing Catalog of Books	B00/99	$1.50
☐	The Technique of Porcupine Quill Decoration /Orchard	B00/01	$8.95
☐	In Hardback	B99/01	$15.95
☐	The Technique of North American Indian Beadwork /Smith	B00/02	$10.95
☐	In Hardback	B99/02	$15.95
☐	Techniques of Beading Earrings by Deon DeLange	B00/03	$7.95
☐	More Techniques of Beading Earrings by Deon DeLange	B00/04	$8.95
☐	America's *First* First World War: The French & Indian	B00/05	$8.95
☐	Crow Indian Beadwork/Wildschut and Ewers	B00/06	$8.95
☐	New Adventures in Beading Earrings by Laura Reid	B00/07	$8.95
☐	North American Indian Burial Customs by Dr. H. C. Yarrow	B00/09	$9.95
☐	Traditional Indian Crafts by Monte Smith	B00/10	$8.95
☐	Traditional Indian Bead & Leather Crafts / Smith/VanSickle	B00/11	$9.95
☐	Indian Clothing of the Great Lakes: 1740-1840 /Hartman	B00/12	$9.95
☐	In Hardback	B99/12	$15.95
☐	Shinin' Trails: A Possibles Bag of Fur Trade Trivia by Legg	B00/13	$7.95
☐	Adventures in Creating Earrings by Laura Reid	B00/14	$9.95
☐	Circle of Power by William Higbie	B00/15	$7.95
☐	In Hardback	B99/15	$13.95
☐	Etienne Provost: Man of the Mountains by Jack Tykal	B00/16	$9.95
☐	In Hardback	B99/16	$15.95
☐	A Quillwork Companion by Jean Heinbuch	B00/17	$9.95
☐	In Hardback	B99/17	$15.95
☐	Making Indian Bows & Arrows...The Old Way /Wallentine	B00/18	$9.95
☐	Making Arrows...The Old Way by Doug Wallentine	B00/19	$4.00
☐	Hair of the Bear: Campfire Yarns & Stories by Eric Bye	B00/20	$9.95
☐	How To Tan Skins The Indian Way by Evard Gibby	B00/21	$4.50
☐	A Beadwork Companion by Jean Heinbuch	B00/22	$10.95
☐	Beads and Cabochons by Patricia Lyman	B00/23	$9.95

• •

At your local bookstore or use this handy form for ordering :

EAGLE'S VIEW PUBLISHING READERS SERVICE, DEPT B&C
6756 North Fork Road - Liberty, Utah 84310

Please send me the above title(s). I am enclosing $_____ (Please add $2.50 per order to cover shipping and handling.) Send check or money order - no cash or C.O.D.s please.

Ms./Mrs./Mr. _____

Address _____

City/State/Zip Code _____

Prices and availability subject to change without notice. Allow three to four weeks for delivery.